Be/

A HYMN LOVER'S DIARY

C. P. HANCOCK

Author of

My Friend George

A Hymn Lovers' Companion etc.

ISBN 0 9509378 1 9

Orphans Press Leominster

SOME CONTEMPORARY AUTHORS OF OUR HYMNS

Rev. and Mrs. Christopher Idle
A happy informal picture

Rev. Father Brian Foley

Rev. Caryl Micklem

Bishop T. Dudley-Smith

Rev. F. Pratt-Green
with his newly awarded M.B.E. Medal

CONTENTS

My thanks to all who have encouraged and helped me in the production of this little book. I owe a special debt of gratitude to my wife and my good friend Alec Bryers for all the hard work they have put in and the many suggestions, corrections and Alec for preparing the typescript for publication.

The Laurels,   C. P. Hancock.
   Porlock,
      Somerset.

A HYMN LOVER'S DIARY

PREFACE

It is now over ten years since my previous book 'A HYMN LOVERS COMPANION' was produced. In spite of fears, it enjoyed a modest success and many who read it kindly suggested that I should follow it with another on the same subject. For a long time I could not see how this could be done - if I simply used the former chronological framework there would be a lot of tedious repetition - so the whole idea was shelved. The subject still lay dormant in my mind, until it suddenly clicked - 'A HYMN LOVER'S DIARY' - where the only chronology would be my own life - the hymns that made an impact on me from my earliest days until now.

One review of the former book deftly described it as "an informal series of potted biographies from Ambrose to Appleford (not forgetting Anon!)". This much I hope to do again; but simply around the framework of my own experience and reactions. It follows that this book will be more personal and subjective than the last and will naturally reflect the experience of one brought up in a small but lively Methodist Church. I hope this will not detract from its value; so, dear reader, whatever opinions I express that you disagree with, blame it on me alone!

When I wrote the previous book I inserted the numbers in the Methodist Hymn Book (1933) as references, hoping that readers using other hymnals would not be put off by this - and indeed they were not, for the book has circulated among all the mainstream denominations. I sincerely hope and pray that this may be repeated. So I have repeated this practice, except that the numbers will now refer mainly to 'HYMNS & PSALMS'.

One further point: where there is only a passing reference to an author it usually means that his/her life has been more fully told in 'A HYMN

LOVERS COMPANION'.

Younger readers may find the early pages lacking in interest - simply as old man's nostalgia; well, skip them - you will soon come to hymns that will probably live for ever, even if they are already old.

I am aware that some may say "Who does he think he is, that he thinks we should be interested in *his* diary?" I can only say that I hope I am typical of many more; and in any case the little book "THE DIARY OF A NOBODY" was a best seller not so long ago!

But seriously, the previous book has been used for straightforward reading, for reference, for compiling addresses, and some readers have even found it helpful in their daily devotions. If this little book achieves this, I shall have cause to thank God once again.

I therefore offer this further volume, convinced that there is at least as much interest, if not more, in the authors and the circumstances of the composing of hymns. Hymn singing effectively contradicts those who assert that this is a post-Christian era. Also hymns are one of the most powerful ecumenical forces. A glance through any hymn book bears this out. Looking through a Catholic hymnal, I found Wesley, Peronnet, Newton, Baker and other surprising names; and all books have the works of Newman, Faber and - coming up to date - Brian Foley. May God further this process of growing together and together conquering the world.

Chapter 1

CHILDHOOD

I know that memories of our early years can become distorted, but on the whole I think impressions made in extreme youth are very durable. I was blest with a good Christian home, and although we lived in the age of oil lamps and earth closets* and for most of my childhood there was a war on (1914-18) during which two of my brothers were killed, I was too young to realise the sadness and stress my parents were under. Yet they must have done their utmost to make me happy; I honour them for this.

My first recollection of hymns was of one of my older sisters bringing home a copy of the 1911 new Methodist School Hymn Book and showing me the section headed 'God in Nature'. I remember even then not being particularly impressed by most of the numbers - a prejudice that has remained with me.

I did, however, like 'Little beams of rosy light', though I suspect that I was attracted by the pretty tune 'Cottingham' by George B. Blanchard (of whom more later). The words were by that prolific writer of hymns, *FANNY CROSBY,* who is more associated with hymns of the 'Sankey' type, but who did in fact write many children's hymns. We shall meet her again also.

Strangely the hymns of *ANN and JANE TAYLOR* were more successful with me, although they now seem dreadfully dated and are almost completely discarded. Yet Ann's 'God is in heaven, can He hear a little prayer like mine?' is one whose influence was then, and still is, quite relevant to me. Here again, J. H. Maunder's tune had something to do with its original impression on me. I still like his music ("Oh dreadful taste!")

Another author whose name is not associated with children's hymns is *FRANCES RIDLEY HAVERGAL,* but from quite early days her 'God

---

* *and, of course, no radio or television*

1

will take care of you all through the day' produced a comfortable feeling of security in my young consciousness, the smoothly-running tune 'Wentworth' no doubt helping. The latter was written by one J. A. Rogers of whom I know nothing.

I did not have much connection with Sunday School until I was about ten, as we lived a long way from the Church; so I went to morning service with my parents and that was all. But my older sisters were both learning to play keyboards, so I got to know the School hymnal fairly well from their playing.

GEORGE B. BLANCHARD

I have already mentioned G. B. Blanchard's tunes. There were also some examples of words and music by him. One of these which particularly appealed to me was:

> 'Who is the stranger, kingly and kind,
>   Knocking and waiting entrance to find?
> What mean the thorns on His forehead entwined?
>   Listen! He calleth thee.'

This is obviously based on the text 'Behold I stand at the door and knock', with the familiar picture by Holman Hunt 'The Light of the World' in mind. In fact, Blanchard calls his tune 'Holman'.

But who was this George Blanchard? This is the sort of question that will be asked repeatedly throughout this book, simply because in so many instances the life and experience of the author illuminates the hymn, and vice versa.

He was born in 1868 and died in 1926; and devoted all his time to his home Methodist Church in Hull as organist, choirmaster, youth leader, trustee and I imagine anything else that was needed - in fact a general dogsbody! He was a musician of considerable talent, yet he would willingly turn his hand to anything. What a valuable man to have in any Church! How they must have missed him when in later life he had to move to Weston-Super-Mare, where I imagine his many gifts would soon be put to good use, for again we hear of him taking on the post of organist.

As a composer, George's music was tuneful and appealing. It seems a pity that so much of it is forgotten, yet his name lives on in the dignified music to Kipling's 'Recessional'. He calls his tune simply 'Lest we forget'. I have a vivid memory of this tune: I was working during the Second

2

World war at an inland Naval Training Camp; the lads paraded in the square every morning, but this one was particularly unpleasant, with bitterly freezing fog making them invisible to me. Then through the fog came the stately and bold tones of the 'ship's' band playing 'Lest we forget'. This it seems was a regular item of their repertoire.

HENRY BURTON

Another author whose hymns bring back childhood memories is Henry Burton who, too, is remembered today by one hymn 'There's a light upon the mountains' (246 H. & P.). This hymn has survived two world wars, although I have always felt that it has the over-optimistic tone typical of the turn of the century; and yet the words are still an inspiring celebration of the "New fact of our time" - as Dr. Temple calls it - The World Church and its incredible growth.

Henry Burton was born in 1840 at Swannington, in Leicestershire, to devout Methodist parents, and the family emigrated to America while he was a boy. He graduated at Beloit College and was trained for the ministry. After having charge of a Church in Wisconsin he returned to England where he ministered in Lancashire and then in London. Unfortunately he had a serious breakdown in health at the age of sixty-four, had to retire and could not work again, although he lived until he was nearly ninety.

It is, however, Dr. Burton's hymns for children that I remember from this time. These were written in his younger days and are expressive of an energetic and ebullient personality. Does this one illustrate his own youthful conversion?

> 'The world is full of singing -
> I hear it everywhere,
> The flowers their bells are ringing
> Out in the scented air;
> And up above, around me
> The silent anthems roll,
> *For the glorious Lord has found me*
> And there's music in my soul.'

The attractive music which matches the words is by Rev. W. F. Moulton, a pupil of the distinguished organist A. H. Mann, formerly of King's College, Cambridge, and composer, among many other things, of many fine hymn tunes.

On a different level are Dr. Burton's hymns on Christian conduct, written with young people in mind. I will quote parts of just one:-

'Have you had a kindness shown?
Pass it on.

• • • • • • •

'Have you found the heavenly light?
Pass it on!'

Recently during Advent we sang "There's a light upon the mountains" and I found it strangely relevant and prophetic. Who could have predicted the end of the "Cold War" with its terrifying threat of atomic arms? Or who would have dared to think that South Africa could have become a democracy under a former political prisoner without suffering a bloodbath? Or what shall we say of the peace process in Northern Ireland and the hope of peace between those ancient enemies - Jew and Arab?

Indeed, "He is breaking down the barriers, He is casting up the way,
He is calling for His angels to build up the gates of day,
But his angels here are human, not the shining hosts above,
And the drumbeats of His army are the heartbeats of our love."

Chapter 2

SCHOOL DAYS

I am now jumping a few years. My memories are now connected with Sunday School as well as Church. Of course day school ran alongside these, but the standard of singing here was deplorable. The Head was a good player, but when he was conducting prayers one of the lady teachers usually 'played'. None of them could do more than play the air with what seemed to me like a few random discords here and there. Keble's 'New every morning' (636 H. & P.) came up regularly, occasionally varied by one or two others, including 'O Jesus I have promised' (704 H. & P.). Although the meaning of the words escaped me, I always liked the tune - J. W. Elliot's 'Day of Rest'. I was sorry when this was swept away with a lot more Victoriana, but I'm glad this old war-horse is now reinstated. (The tendency is one we shall come across later).

It was in Church much later that the meaning of this great hymn dawned on me, and later still that I discovered the origin of it. The author, *Rev. J. E. BODE* (1816-74) was the son of a Post Office official, who was able to be educated at Eton, Charterhouse and Oxford, where he had a distinguished career. After ordination he was Rector of Westwell, Oxon., and later of Castle Camps, Cambridgeshire, both quite obscure parishes. It was in the latter that this hymn was written.

The occasion was the confirmation of his daughter and two sons. I think we can imagine the thrill of singing their own hymn, written by their father, as these young people - presumably in company with others from the parish - made their solemn vows. The hymn is based on Luke 9, v.57: 'I will follow You wheresoever You go'. On that occasion they would have sung two extra verses, one of which was dropped soon after, but the other - the final one - we used to sing and I regret this is now usually omitted:

5

'O let me see Thy footmarks
    And in them plant my own;
My hope to follow duly
    Is in Thy strength alone.
O guide me, call me, draw me,
    Uphold me to the end,
And then in heaven receive me,
    My Saviour and my Friend.'

A good finale, certainly.

In searching out the lives of the people who have given us our hymns, I have sometimes been surprised how many gifted men like John Bode seemed content to live and die in out-of-the-way places when there must have been advancements for the ambitious. He was, after all, elected to the Bampton lectureship in 1855 - an honour indeed, earned only by the more outstanding theologians, funded a century earlier by the will of Rev. John Bampton. He was also the author of several books, yet apparently content with his cure of what must have been a rather unrewarding parish with its small population, well away from the Church. It is a good thing that some are so happy in their job that they are content to let preferment pass them by.

+ + + + +

In due course I progressed to Grammar School, where morning prayers were quite different. Again the Head conducted them, not in the quiet, reverent voice to which I had been accustomed, but in an over-bearing, booming voice with which he would gallop through the General Thanksgiving at such a pace that I never *did* get the fine words until the odd occasion when the Deputy Head read it in more measured style. ... But we should be talking about hymns!

Well, we used the old edition of 'Hymns Ancient and Modern', having a fairly varied diet of hymns, some of which were new to me and some had a verse or two that were unfamiliar. *KEBLE*'s 'There is a book who runs may read' (340 H. & P.) is one. At school we sang an unfamiliar, but picturesque verse:-

'The moon above, the Church below,
    A wondrous race they run,
But all their radiance, all their glow,
    Each borrows from its sun.'

With this verse or not, this hymn has stuck with me all my life, the last verse especially. From youthful ramblings on the lovely Malvern Hills I used to aim for a little shelter erected, I think, in memory of one of the Somers family (for Midsummer Hill was then on their estate - now National Trust). Fixed inside was a plaque with this verse on it:-

'Thou who hast given me eyes to see
And love this sight so fair,
Give me a heart to find out Thee,
And read Thee everywhere.'

One day I went to this almost sacred spot and the shelter had gone, plaque and all. My disappointment was intense; where had it gone? Some years later I found it on the churchyard wall at Eastnor (the estate Church). I hope some day it can be replaced on the hill where the view is as superb as ever.

There is another regret concerning this lovely hymn of 'God revealed in Nature.' Why have we been deprived of the grand tune 'St. Flavian' which has been wedded to these words for generations? The 'Companion to Hymns & Psalms' tries to justify this, quite ineffectually.

LEWIS HENSLEY

If I am asked which hymn, new to me through school prayers, had the most lasting effect on me, without any hesitation it would be 'Thy kingdom come, O God' (783 H. & P.). Inexplicably, seeing it was first published in 1867, it was not in the 1904 MHB, and it seems that all the Free Churches were slow to adopt such a treasure. I think a lot of nonsense has been talked and written about the Victorian age - that the Church had no problem about morals, or that in its prosperity it closed its eyes to poverty, crime and the other abuses of its time. It is not my present aim to quote historical denials of these assumptions, but here we have a Victorian clergyman concerned about the tyrannies of sin, hatred, war, oppression, lust, crime and the rest. It is true we no longer sing the dramatic verse:

'Men scorn Thy sacred name,
And wolves devour Thy fold:
By many deeds of shame
We learn that love grows cold.'

Pity! Also since the B.B.C. published their Hymn Book (1957) we do not sing:

7

'O'er heathen lands afar thick darkness broodeth yet'

but: 'O'er lands both near and far . . . . .'

This is at least honest, for we have learned that we Christians are often less devoted to our faith than Jews, Moslems or Hindus - shame on us!

Just a little personal appreciation of this hymn. I find, in saying the Lord's Prayer to myself, that many of the phrases are so full of meaning and have such wide implications that they need a pause and some meditation. One of these is 'Thy kingdom come'. I find it helpful to repeat to myself some verses of this hymn. I can only suggest - try it.

So what of the author, Lewis Hensley (1824-1905)? Like John Bode he was brilliant at school and University - except that he was a Cambridge man - but unlike him his gifts seemed naturally to lead him to preferment. He was Senior Wrangler and Smith's Prizeman, and he remained at Trinity College as Fellow and Tutor. After ordination at the age of 27 he held two curacies, then a minor living, before being appointed Vicar of Hitchin, where he remained to be Rural Dean and Honorary Canon of St. Albans Cathedral. He died suddenly in a train in the county where he was born, Norfolk, aged 81. So ended a long and fruitful life, in which he also published two books of hymns and two devotional books.

+   +   +   +   +

During my Grammar School days I was so overloaded with homework that although I went to Church on Sunday and was nominally in the choir, I could never go to choir practice during term; but I was tolerated, as a callow youth whose voice was breaking - not much use, but no harm either.

Hymns were still making a gradual impression on me during this period. I remember for the first time being confronted with 'O come, O come, Immanuel' (85 H. & P.) one Sunday, after being absent from practice. I was carried along by the others who knew it and it made an instant impression on me. I knew nothing about plainsong - and indeed this is not pure plainsong (the refrain 'Rejoice, rejoice' departs from it), but I liked this too. In some mysterious way, as I joined in, I had the feeling of joining in the praises and prayers of Christians down the ages. The tune dates back to the fifteenth century, but who can say how much older it is? A good deal of controversy has raged over the origins of this ancient hymn, but it is known that the custom of singing 'The seven O's, at

Advent dates back to the ninth century, possibly earlier, but they were only rendered in metrical form much later - even the eighteenth century; and in the next century *Dr. J. M. NEALE,* that great researcher and translator of Latin hymns, made the present version. Whatever the truth about the words or music, I still get this feeling of oneness with my ancestors of the faith whenever I sing it.

Chapter 3

CAROL SINGING

One activity in which I was able to participate in Grammar School days was carol singing. School finished well before Christmas; and at Church we had a choir whose enthusiasm exceeded its size, so days - even weeks - before Christmas, we went all over the neighbourhood singing on behalf of the National Children's Home. We sang the classical carols, of course: 'Hark the herald angels sing', 'O come all ye faithful' and such like; but there were three that especially appealed to me.

You may think the choice odd, but the fact remains and I still enjoy them. 'It came upon the midnight clear' (108 H. & P.) is an established favourite, written by *EDMUND H. SEARS,* (1810-1876), an influential American Unitarian minister. Now Unitarians have given us many fine hymns. We shall meet them again later, so this may be a good place to define their views.

Unitarianism has existed in isolated cases for many centuries; in fact there are records of people being martyred for denying the Holy Trinity and the divinity of Jesus Christ in quite early times; but by the seventeenth century there were many groups who felt they did not want to be bound by rigid creeds. In the eighteenth century controversy boiled up on a large scale in England, and as the penal laws against them were relaxed a number of men under the leadership of the great scientist Joseph Priestley began actively propagating their doctrines. Basically these only required one to believe there was a God and to lead a good moral life. They claimed freedom from dogmas of any kind, so they tended to vary a good deal between regarding Jesus as simply a great teacher and a perfect example, to believing in Him as divine and worthy of worship. Edmund Sears was of the latter class and like all his brethren he had a strong belief in the social implications of the gospel.

So what appealed to me about this hymn in my youth? The poetic element undoubtedly: 'Angels bending near the earth to touch their harps of gold' and 'Ever o'er its Babel sounds the blessed angels sing' and - even more impressive - 'Beneath the angel strain have rolled two thousand years of wrong . . . O hush the noise, ye men of strife, and hear the angels sing'. Unfortunately the last verse has been altered, to exclude (so we are told) controversial humanist references, but I miss 'the prophet bards', 'the age of gold' and the 'ancient splendours' of peace. Never mind, it's still a good hymn in spite of substituting dull office English for superb poetry.

The tune is a good one, admirably suiting the words. The first part is a traditional Herefordshire melody which can be found in the English Hymnal under the name 'Eardisley' (incidentally, if you are in that district call it Urds-ley and you will be accepted as educated). The rest of the tune is entirely Sullivan's composition.

The next carol that has appealed to me from carol singing days until now is 'O little town of Bethlehem' (113 H. & P.). This was written by a really remarkable man - another American - *Bishop PHILLIPS BROOKS* (1835-93). If all his biographers have written about him is true, I should love to have known him. 6'6" tall (some say only 6'4") and well built in proportion, with an open-hearted manner that attracted all - educated, ordinary or simple, even children. To prove the latter point, a little story: a woman who had just heard the news of his death could not restrain a few tears when her five-year-old daughter said, "Don't cry, think how happy the angels will be!"

"Impressive as a giant - radiant as an angel," said one admirer. Another, more theologically minded, put it this way: "Most preachers take a bucket or half a bucket of the Word of God and attempt to convey to their congregation its truth; but this man is a great water-main attached to the reservoir of God's grace and love."

This carol has all the vividness and immediacy of an eye-witness account, and it had been thought - and said - that it was written actually as he looked over Bethlehem on Christmas night; but no, he wrote it some two years later for his Sunday School; but the view and the magical feeling associated with it were still so clear in his mind that he could still write "How still we see thee lie" as if he were still there.

It is strange that a ten-talent man like this should have been unpromising in his youth, for he trained as a teacher and quite soon felt himself to be a failure at the job. Just how the call to the ministry came at this low ebb in his life we are not told, but this was his God-chosen work in life. Thus he trained for the Episcopal Church and was called to several important pastorates; and after refusing a professorship he accepted the post of Bishop of Massachusetts - one that still brought him into constant touch with the ordinary people he loved.

The last choice of carol that has stuck with me is probably not quite so widely known, but just as appealing: 'Cradled in a manger' (98 H. & P.). One of the verses that early impressed me runs:-

'Blessed Saviour, Christ most holy,
In a manger Thou didst rest;
Canst Thou stoop again yet lower,
And abide within my breast?

Evil things are there before Thee;
In the heart, where they have fed,
Wilt Thou pitifully enter,
Son of man, and lay Thy head?'

This is reminiscent of the previous carol:

'O Holy Child of Bethlehem,
Descent to us, we pray;
Cast out our sin, and enter in;
Be born in us today!'

'Cradled in a manger' is perhaps rather more childish, but I was only a child when I first heard it and I hope I am still childlike enough to appreciate it. In any event, the author - the *Rev. GEORGE ROWE* (1830-1913) - wrote these verses with children in mind, as indeed he did all the hymns he wrote.

Mr. Rowe's two great loves were children and overseas missionary work. It is therefore not surprising that he was Editor of the children's magazine 'At Home and Abroad' for many years. This hymn first appeared in a Christmas number of the magazine. He also wrote the biographies of several missionary pioneers of a generation before his time, and many devotional books much prized in his day. After serving in various Circuits he was appointed Professor of Pastoral Theology at Headingly College. The tune was composed for these words by the Rev. Sidney Dunman, who composed several hymn tunes but is only remembered by this one 'St. Winifred'. Other tunes have been set to the hymn, but so far none has dislodged this one that now seems 'wedded'.

Let me end with another quotation, which demonstrates the author's interest in world missions:

'And to those who never listened
To the message of Thy birth,
Who have winter, but no Christmas
Bringing them Thy peace on earth,
Send to these the joyful tidings;
By all people, in each home,
Be there heard the Christmas anthem:
Praise to God, the Christ has come!'

+ + + + +

I remember when I was young, after a long marathon of carol singing I had had enough, so that when preachers wanted to continue singing them for a few more Sundays I tended to rebel! I still welcome New Year hymns.

Chapter 4

BOYHOOD IN CHURCH

I recently received a postcard from an Anglican clergyman friend of mine, on holiday in Cornwall: it was a view of Land's End. On the back he asked me if I remembered *CHARLES WESLEY*'s lines, 'Lo! on a narrow neck of land 'twixt two unbounded seas I stand' which, he thought, were written on that very spot. I hunted through my old copy of the 1904 MHB (which we were using at this point in my 'diary') and found the hymn beginning 'Thou God of glorious majesty'. It goes on: 'A point of time, a moment's space, removes me to the heavenly place, or shuts me up in hell'. I was not too clear about the figure Wesley had in mind - which sea was it? When I next met my friend I quoted these lines. He said with a twinkle, "Don't suppose you Methodists sing that sort of thing now!" He was right; we don't.

I thought of another hymn that survived into the 1933 MHB, by that mildest of all the Oxford Movement men, *JOHN KEBLE*, which reads 'Save, Lord, by love or fear' (276 MHB). Looking back to those distant days there were a few - very few - preachers who liked to 'dangle us over the pit' and they were mostly from outside our denomination. I suppose they thought we Methodists needed that sort of thing! This all set me thinking, and I thought all the harder when our preacher one Sunday evening quoted old Dr. *SAMUEL JOHNSON*'s fear of 'being damned and shut up in hell'. "Of course, we no longer believe that now," he declared. He preached the love of God, but did not explain how the references to hell in the New Testament were to be explained (or explained away).

Now the evening congregation at that church was the small one of the day, but consisted of the more thoughtful members of the Church (fairly typical, I should think), so as it was my turn next Sunday, I determined to tackle the subject while this controversial sermon was fresh in their minds. Rather to my surprise there was general gratitude that someone had tackled this thorny subject . . . But I digress - I don't think the odd sermon of this type did me any psychological harm and even now I wonder if I was saved by fear before I experienced love.

So . . . back to hymns. The nearest thing of this sort to survive to the present day is *EDWARD CASWALL*'s translation of the Spanish sonnet (formerly attributed to St. Francis Xavier) rendered into Latin in the seventeenth century by a Jesuit priest (who incidentally ascribed the original to St. Francis):

> 'My God, I love Thee - not because
> I hope for heaven thereby,
> Nor yet because who love Thee not
> Are lost eternally'.   (171 H. & P.)

It is notable that the last line has been softened from Caswall's original, 'Must burn eternally', which is a strictly literal translation of the Latin. This marks a significant modification of our theology, although a century ago many thinkers, like Charles Kingsley, refused to accept any view which contradicted his favourite text, 'God is Love', which is inscribed on his tombstone. I think it is significant that St. Paul in his Epistles, while insisting on judgement, does not dwell on 'hell' or 'fire'. He was the earliest writer in the New Testament and his view is good enough for me.

OLIVER WENDELL HOLMES

We now turn to a varied selection of hymns, which because of their quality have endured from my childhood and still have a relevance today; they all made an early impression on me and still do. The first is 'Lord of all being, throned afar' (11 H. & P.). The author, Oliver Wendell Holmes (1809-94), lived in America when bigger and better telescopes, (although small by modern standards) were probing deeper and deeper into the universe. With his Christian faith he pictured God as Creator and Lord of the boundless galaxies being revealed in his day. The first lines set the tone:-

> 'Lord of all being, throned afar,
> Thy glory flames from sun and star,
> Centre and soul of every sphere . . .'

So far, so good; in a few words he has whirled us through space, spanning the universe to express the Glory of God, making us bow humbly before Him Who planned it all,—infinitely beyond our comprehension. Then, what a contrast! We come in a split second from infinity right back to the heart of human need: 'Yet to each loving heart how near' - a marvellous verse to recite while contemplating the sky on a bright starry night. Based as it is on Isaiah 57, v.15: 'I dwell in the high and holy place, and with him who is of a broken and humble spirit', we have here the same dramatic jump from the infinite to the intimate.

The hymn goes on to relate the natural phenomena - sun, stars, midnight, noon and the rainbow - to our spiritual life, ending with 'All, save the clouds of sin, are Thine'. I find this picture particularly vivid. As I am writing this on a bright autumn day, it is pleasantly warm while the sun shines; but let a cloud obscure it for a few minutes and the promise of a frosty night to follow sends a shiver down the spine - the contrast between the warmth of God's presence and the chill of doubt and unbelief.

What kind of a man was this who could first overwhelm us with infinity, then reassure us of God's immanence? He certainly was a remarkable man. Son of the minister of the First Congregational Church, Cambridge, Mass., and a brilliant lad, he graduated in medicine and the arts at Harvard University, went to Europe for further study and after several prestigious appointments, finally accepted the Chair of Professor of Anatomy at his old University.

Running parallel with his professional career, he developed a love of writing on general topics and began contributing to various periodicals. He even founded one, the 'Atlantic Monthly', for which he wrote most of his articles. His writings began to bring him fame on both sides of the Atlantic, although few had any idea what his real profession was. First a series 'The autocrat at the breakfast table', then 'The professor at the breakfast table' (from which this poem is taken). 'The poet at the breakfast table' and 'Over the teacups' followed. His active mind ranged over countless subjects (and sometimes nothing in particular) with engaging wit and piercing perception. A few quotations will suffice to illustrate his style: 'Man has his will, but woman has her way'; 'A moment of insight is sometimes worth a life's experience'; and amazingly for a man who had never known amplified sound or jet planes, 'Silence, like a poultice, comes to heal the blows of sound'; and typically 'To be seventy years young is sometimes far more hopeful than to be forty years old'. This from a man who did not resign his University post until he was seventy-three!

Professor Holmes was brought up, as we have seen, in the Congregational Church, but he became uneasy with what Whittier called 'the iron creed' of strict Calvinism so often preached at that time, and he joined the Unitarians, although he was never quite in line with them either. He defined his position as always clinging to the love of God as revealed in Jesus Christ. Of his relations with his fellow Unitarians he said in his teasing, enigmatic way, "I believe more than some and less than others - I like those who believe more, more than those who believe less". Certainly in later life he treasured the great evangelical hymns "finding in them a strength lacking in those of my own communion". His old age was not only active but very rewarding, honours being showered on him by Universities the world over. He retained the wonderful ability to be able to concentrate his mind on what he was doing to the complete detachment from any other subject at that time. A friend visiting him at the great age of eighty-four found him "the chirpiest old man I have ever known".

Although he wrote several hymns, this is his best-known by far and he says of it in his magnanimous way, "I hope that people may forget the differences in the lines of truth that we see through our human prisms, and join in singing (inwardly) this hymn to the Source of Light we all need to lead us, and the warmth which alone can make us brothers". What a plea for charity, what a message of peace! Needed as much now as it was then.

There are two words here that I would like to dwell on. The first is 'inwardly'. I have suggested using this hymn under the starry sky, so we need to commit it to memory, although I prefer to say learn it by heart, or as Holmes says, inwardly - part of our consciousness that can surface when we need it, under the night sky, in illness or sleeplessness, or as I have previously indicated, to enlarge upon a petition in our prayers.

The other word is 'light' - emanating from the supreme source of light, God Himself. Both these thoughts form a connecting link between this hymn and the next, which is another I find easy to remember, bringing a great sense of indebtedness to God for the salvation offered to us in Jesus Christ.

THOMAS BINNEY

I refer to 'Eternal Light' (458 H. & P.) by Dr. Thomas Binney. This was written on a bright starlight night as the thought came to him, not outside, but from his study window at Newport as he watched the sun set and the stars appear. The thought came to him that light is eternal, as God is eternal. He could see this because the night was crystal clear, but when clouds obscured the sun and stars, the light was still there above the clouds. The affinity of this hymn with 'Lord of all being' is obvious.

Thomas Binney (born in Newcastle-on-Tyne in 1798) worked long hours for a bookseller, soon developing a love for books; and by continuous reading he educated himself. He entered Coward College to train for the Congregational ministry and did well, yet no-one seemed to realise that here was a student of exceptional talents until he was appointed to his first charge in Bedford, and later at Newport (I.O.W.) where his attraction for young men was soon evident. At the age of thirty-one the call to serve in London came and he took charge of King's Weigh House Chapel where he spent the rest of his ministry, being acknowledged as the foremost preacher in the Capital. He had no time for the affected, academic style of preaching prevalent in his day, but used ordinary speech to great effect; and he is mainly remembered, apart from his dynamic preaching, for his constant advocacy of the better ordering of nonconformist services and for his trenchant attacks on the Anglican Church's abuses. He made some enemies among the clergy ("Who does he think he is, an outsider, criticising us?"), yet many of the men in the Church who saw the need for reforms welcomed the help of this unanswerable ally. So great was the respect in which he was held that many leaders of the Anglican Church were present at his funeral, Dean Stanley taking part. In the days prior to his death he was often heard to repeat the verse:

'O how shall I, whose native sphere
is dark, whose mind is dim,
Before the Ineffable appear,
And on my naked spirit bear
The uncreated beam?'

In my experience, this is a hymn which increases in value as the years go by. It not only did so with the author, but both my father and father-in-law - nonagenarian and centenarian respectively - had made it their own to such an extent that they both expressed a wish for it to be sung at their funerals. I can feel the same thing happening to me!

AUGUSTUS TOPLADY

I sometimes think I could write a book (yes, another!) on the mythology of hymns. Stories have gathered around some of them, their

18

writers and the circumstances of their composition that are often difficult to verify - or even complete fabrications. I have always tried to view all stories with a healthy scepticism, but even so I have been found guilty of propagating a few errors! The one about the writing of 'Rock of Ages' is one I have never fallen for. Even dear old Arthur Mee, who I had always imagined stuck to the truth, has been taken in by this - "really, Arthur, you should have done what I did - got out of your car and tried to fit yourself into that famous cleft in the rock" - so the seeds of doubt were sown in my mind. I had been led to understand that the author, Augustus Toplady, was trudging down Burrington Combe when an awful thunderstorm broke over him; seeing this cleft which has become known as the Rock of Ages, he sheltered in there. Feeling, as a Christian might, the security of his position, these lines came to his mind. One version goes one better: groping in his pockets for pencil and paper, lest the inspiration of the moment might pass, he could find no paper when, providentially, he saw a playing card at his feet and scrawled down these immortal lines. It was a relief when, years later, I read in a sober book "There seems to be no foundation for the picturesque story that Toplady composed . . etc." The fact seems to be that the story was put about by the owner of the estate on which the rock is situated, over a century later than the supposed event.

So, after demolishing the legend, where do we look for the inspiration of these verses? Well, it could have been quite an original idea, but Charles Wesley had already written a hymn 'Rock of Israel, cleft for me'. Did Toplady know this? In any event the idea is different, based as it is on the story of Moses striking the rock in the desert and water gushing out to slake the thirst of the desperate Israelites. It *is* possible that Toplady was recalling the incident at Burrington, but in fact the hymn was written twelve years later - at least the first four lines; the rest followed later still. It is generally thought that he was quoting Isaiah 26, v.4: 'The Lord Jehovah is the Rock of Ages'. You will not find this translation in your King James (A.V.) which was the only version used in Toplady's time, where it is rendered rather inadequately 'The Lord Jehovah is everlasting strength'. So where did he get this picturesque translation, one that was not picked up until the Revised Version, well over a hundred years later? The only conclusion must be that Toplady read Hebrew and possessed a Hebrew Old Testament. If this is so he was not the empty-headed ranter he has sometimes been represented to be.

These remarks apply equally well to many of the old fellows of the eighteenth century. Not that anyone would be likely to accuse the

Wesleys of being empty-headed, but I have been astonished to find evidences of how they anticipated modern translations in their hymns. JOHN NEWTON is a different case, not so highly thought of, but he did just the same. We shall come to them in due course.

To get back to the 'Rock of Ages', we know something of its composition. In 1775 Toplady contributed an article to the 'Gospel Magazine', entitled 'Life, a journey', under the nom-de-plume 'Minimus', which ended with the four first lines 'Rock of Ages, cleft for me . . .' Later he took over this magazine as editor - I imagine he made it more Calvinistic in tone - and within a year published (this time under assumed initials) a wordy and extraordinary article comparing sins (a formidable list!) which anyone might be expected to commit in their lifetime, with the National Debt: both astronomical and unpayable! He ended this outburst with the complete hymn 'Rock of Ages, cleft for me'.

Solemn and impressive, it is perhaps not a hymn for everyday use, yet it lives and will live as long as we transgress God's will and sincerely seek His forgiveness. The ranting article is forgotten, and that was more typical of the author. As a Calvinist he was urging man's total depravity as the need for Christ's all-atoning work, but he was also getting in a swipe at Wesley who preached that the Gospel was for all, and no-one, however bad, was beyond its reach. The war of words that went on between these two great men of God is best forgotten, but there is no doubt that Wesley came out as the more charitable of the two. It has been truly said that this hymn is a case of the wrath of man praising God.

It is noticeable that Toplady did not adopt his narrow, bitter Calvinistic views at first. Brought up by his mother - tragically widowed by war when the boy was only a year old - we can only wonder what sacrifices she had to make for him. For reasons we do not know, they had to move from their home in Farnham to Ireland. She managed to send him to Trinity College, Dublin, where he graduated M.A. We assume Hebrew was one of his subjects. Again mysteriously, he went to a Methodist service in a barn in an out-of-the-way part of Ireland and was converted. He speaks rather disparagingly of the event: "Strange that I, who had sat so long under the means of grace in England, should be brought to God in an obscure part of Ireland by the ministry of one who could hardly spell his own name". This was the beginning of the vitriolic style that was to spoil his witness - especially when he came in contact with Wesley whom - among other things - he called 'Pope John'. Actually the preacher in question did not have a degree, as Toplady had, but had received a good ordinary education: a more charitable assessment of him was "a born orator - yet lowly minded".

It was sad that Toplady adopted the dreadful creed that was so bitingly satirised by Swift:

"We are the chosen few, all others will be damned,
There is no place in heaven for you; we can't have heaven crammed".

It has been urged, charitably, that much of his bitterness was due to the persistent ill-health he suffered, which caused his death at the age of 38, in 1778.

Stories about his passing abound: all testify to a sure and certain faith in the Saviour whose great love could forgive all his sins and fit him for life in his presence. Unfortunately there are some Christians whose difficult personalities tend to make us think: "If they are going to be in heaven, count me out!" Rather we should look more closely at our own lives and ask: "Is there anything in *my* behaviour liable to make anyone think like that?" We believe that God in his love will continue the refining of us all where we have neglected it here.

THOMAS HORNBLOWER GILL

I move on to an author whose hymns are in total contrast to what has gone before. It did not dawn on me that they were all by the same man, for authors' names did not appear under hymns in the 1904 hymn book.

The first is one we no longer have (yes, I am breaking my own rule), but I quote it as an example of this man's verses when he was young:-

'Lord, in the fullness of my might
I would for Thee be strong.'   (396 MHB)

This is a sentiment that appealed to me in my youth and I would have thought it was still valid for the young:-

'I would not with swift-winged zeal
On the world's errands go,
And labour up the heavenly hill
With weary feet and slow.'

As a youngster I found this quite searching, and it led on to the desire:-

'Accept me in my golden time,
In my dear joys have part.
O not for Thee my fading fires,
The ashes of my heart".

21

Fortunately we still have two of this man's more mature hymns - he was, to give him his full name, Thomas Hornblower Gill (1819-1906), a man who had a great regard for his ancestry. In 'We come unto our fathers' God' (453 H. & P.) he develops the thought of God's forgiveness and grace being the same from age to age, because the 'cleaving sins' are always the same however much change and progress has been made. Thomas Gill indeed had an ancestry of which he could be proud - a long line of earnest and distinguished Presbyterians; but his immediate forebears had partly rejected their fathers' faith and had tended towards Unitarianism. Thomas accepted these opinions for a while but he came across a group of Christians whose ancestors had been cruelly persecuted because they were Waldenses (a Protestant sect in Italy). These good people kept alive the memory of their fathers who lived - and in some cases died - for their faith. For some reason be began to read the hymns of Isaac Watts and compared them with the 'shrunken and dwindled presentation' in the mutilated version found in Unitarian hymnals.

His youthful bigotry had led him to reject the opportunity to enter Oxford University as he would not subscribe to the 39 Articles, choosing rather a rigorous course of self-education in the course of which he learned Greek, reading the New Testament in the original tongue.

These three influences combined to bring him back to a full faith in Jesus Christ. He joined the famous Dr. Dale's Church, Carrs Lane, Birmingham, who considered Mr. Gill the greatest living hymn writer and included many of his hymns in a compilation that he made for his own Church. Some hailed him as the Charles Wesley of his day. (I have heard extravagant claims like this for writers of our own day: I think we have to wait to see what the next generation thinks. Thomas Gill has not been treated too kindly by his succeeding generations).

His other well-known hymn 'Lord God, by whom all change is wrought' (39 H. & P.) is based on the saying of St. Augustine: 'Immutabilis mutans omnia' which I would think could be translated 'Unchangeability changing everything'. This paradox is worked out with the originality typical of the man: God the unchangeable, the Spirit who makes all things new.

Mr. Gill lived to the great age of 87, retaining his bright outlook and calm faith, as his friend Dr. Dale put it: "Experiencing a constant vision of God". This does not mean that he never had any trouble, but in his own words: "If clouds came, I prayed and the light returned - it was wonderful". What a recipe for a happy old age!

Chapter 5

YOUTH AND CONVERSION

Yes, I use the term 'conversion' deliberately. It means 'turning round' - and that is just what I did. I suppose I was drifting - drifting away from my upbringing. Probably no-one noticed this movement but I was vaguely aware of it and in my innermost self I didn't want it to happen. The exact means of how I came to turn round is unimportant. It happened in the rather old-fashioned way - 'going up to the front'; but the main thing was that by God's help I had now a new direction.

Hymns were one means of showing what had taken place: what I had simply sung I now experienced. This was a watershed in my life if ever there was one. It is strange, I had never been a Charles Wesley worshipper and I tended to be slightly irritated by older people who were, yet it was his hymns that first came to life at this time. The first to do so was 'O for a thousand tongues to sing my great Redeemer's praise' (744 H. & P.). I remember singing 'His blood can make the foulest clean, His blood availed for me'. I wasn't too sure of the theology, but 'for ME'; whatever it meant it was for ME! Later, when we were again singing this great hymn, I thought one of the greatest bits of compressed theology is in one line: 'He breaks the power of cancelled sin'. Work that one out: justification and sanctification in a few words.

I am not going to launch into a summary of *CHARLES WESLEY*'s life and writings: that has already been done well, and in any case is too big a subject for a book like this. Perhaps my few remarks may stimulate you to follow this up. The hymn just quoted is entitled by Wesley 'For the Anniversary Day of One's Conversion'. The original opening verses made specific reference to the anniversary day, and there were eighteen verses! Thus compilers of hymnals have to make a selection, and I personally am glad that in 'Hymns and Psalms' they have added a verse to provide a more fitting ending; the theme of Christ's offering of Himself was bound to be rather muted, so now we can do that and then let ourselves go with the new conclusion:-

'In Christ our head you then shall know,
Shall feel, your sins forgiven,
Anticipate your heaven below,
And own that love is heaven.

While on the subject of effective climaxes, the last couplet in Wesley's challenging hymn 'A charge to keep I have' (785 H. & P.), 'Assured if I my trust betray, I shall for ever die' has always seemed a negative note on which to end, especially after the word 'assured'; but is the new ending robust and positive enough? See what you think.

The other Wesley hymn that came alive for me was the great 'And can it be' (216 H. & P.) I had to come a long way before I could grasp a truth like 'Amazing love! how can it be that Thou, my God, shouldst die for me?' My faith has been almost entirely subjective (or selfish) - that I should experience God's salvation, the freedom, peace and joy that goes with it, without thinking too much about how all these blessings were won for me. By any standard this is one of the few great hymns: the force of the opening with that question 'And can it be?'; that wonderful piece of what I have called compressed theology 'Emptied Himself of all but love', another illustration of Charles's scholarship. I have already referred to the 18th century writers who could render more vividly dull phrases in the Authorised Version, or even correct mistranslations; and here is another example, this time from the Greek. In Phil. 2: v.7 (A.V.) we read that Christ 'made Himself of no reputation', while Greek scholars tell us that Paul uses a bold word meaning 'emptied Himself'. Have you never, after a spell of hard work, or after a devastating emotional strain, said "I feel utterly drained" or words to that effect? You feel emptied. Paul would teach us the mystery of the atonement: 'emptied' at the incarnation; 'emptied' as He suffered on the Cross. These were the sufferings of our Lord. Wesley's genius crams this into one line *and* adds a bit of his own to make the sacrifice all the more amazing: "Emptied Himself - of all but love".

It might be thought that after the wonderful penultimate verse, making Peter's release from prison a symbol of the new freedom from sin that a Christian feels, another verse must be an anticlimax; but no, he goes on to an even more glorious statement of the assurance that follows this act of release, with Paul's great declaration 'There is therefore now no condemnation for those who are in Christ Jesus', to the confident:-

24

'Bold I approach the eternal throne
And claim the crown, through Christ, my own.'

I do not emphasise the music of these impressive hymns very much, but it has surprised me how universally popular Thomas Campbell's 'Sagina' has become. In my youth, however, this tune was relegated to the 'Appendix' as unsingable, so the words were set to G. C. Martin's 'Holy Faith'. Sadly we no longer have this majestic tune, but it is still a joy to play it from an older book. Try it!

HORATIUS BONAR

I recently returned from a service in which the minister gave a most thoughtful sermon on the text 'I am the door'. The theme was that Jesus Christ was the door through which we enter into new experiences, and gain new insights into old and familiar things. How applicable, I thought, as I returned to writing these memoirs: well-known hymns can take on a totally new aspect, as I have already urged.

Another hymn which has been transformed by MY new point of view was 'Fill Thou my life, O Lord my God, in every part with praise' (792 H. & P.). I used to find myself singing this without much enthusiasm, but as the lines progressed and specific areas of praise were indicated I realised that I ought not to sing them, just because I did not mean them. I became more uneasy as the hymn progressed and when I came to 'So shall no part of day or night from sacredness be free' this was too much. I wanted to have control of at least some of my life, some parts where I could still be boss: I had to stop singing - it was not honest. *NOW* I could sing *and* mean 'But all my life, in every step, be fellowship with Thee.' Of course I know this is an ideal to which we aim, but human nature being what it is, we do not always reach it; yet Divine Grace can, if we let it, help us to progress towards that ideal.

What sort of man was the author and did he always reach his own ideal? He did attain it, for it is difficult to imagine a more dedicated man who crowded his life with effective Christian service: his name - Horatius Bonar (1809-89). The son of an Edinburgh lawyer, he did well at school and entered the University of Edinburgh where he came under the influence of that great Scottish Professor of Theology, Dr. Thomas Chalmers. His dynamic personality was to have a lasting effect on this young student, leading him to become ordained to the ministry of the Church of Scotland. After a spell as an assistant minister he was given the charge of a new parish at Kelso. Here he not only exercised a remarkable ministry, but became widely known for his evangelical tracts, then for his books which appeared almost yearly. In addition he found that increasingly his spiritual advice and help was being sought by correspondence. The secret of his life was that as work increased so the time devoted to prayer increased with it. Thus the guidance he gave was God's will for that particular person in his need.

In contrast with the great care he took over his preaching and counselling, he seems to have thrown off the many hymns he wrote quite casually, so many are now forgotten; but those that survive are of such devotional value that they seem immortal. Other hymns still widely used are 'O Love of God, how strong and true' (42 H. & P.), 'I heard the voice of Jesus say' (136 H. & P.) - and others - but one which has special meaning for me is his communion hymn 'Here, O my Lord, I see Thee face to face' (608 H. & P.). It was often used in my youth but seemed to fall out of favour, then recently we have sung it several times at communion. It brought back some of the blessing of those old times with a new appeal which there must be if our faith is to be kept young. The great hymns have this quality: they can be revived generation after generation and still be valid and effective.

Dr. Bonar did not lead a life free from upheaval and trouble, for he was deeply involved in 'the Disruption' in 1843. This is no place to go into that event, but briefly many churchmen objected to state interference in the appointment of ministers, feeling strongly that the views of church members alone should decide each case. After a few notable cases the whole matter came to a head and, led by the redoubtable Dr. Chalmers, about a third of the ministers withdrew and formed the Free Church of Scotland. This was a desperate step, for they had to build their own churches and manses. Would congregations support them? - that was the question; support was in fact so strong and generosity so great that this was all done. Dr. Bonar had no doubt where his loyalty lay - with his old hero, Dr. Chalmers. He was even co-editor of a new Church newspaper in support of the new Free Church. At the age of 58 he achieved what must have been his cherished ambition, being appointed minister of the Chalmers Memorial Free Church. Happily these old difficulties have long been resolved.

To return to his hymns, even folk who were critical of some of them had to admit that he did a great pioneering work in this field, for he began writing when hymns were anathema, especially in his branch of the Church; but the success of his hymns, written as they were mainly for children, helped a lot to soften this opposition to anything that was not in the Psalms of David. This reveals yet another facet of Dr. Bonar's character: one could imagine him as such a formidable man that children would be scared of him and that he would not understand them at all, but he did; he could see that however much he loved the old Psalter and its dignified tunes, the children were just plain bored, so this was his incentive to write something new and arresting, to catchy tunes they would know. Thus we must think of Dr. Bonar as a real all-rounder. His last assignment was to be elected Moderator of the General Assembly of his Church at the age of 75: his physical stamina as well as his spiritual strength must have been enormous.

SAMUEL DAVIES

It is understandable that at this time, as a new Christian, I should feel the need of hymns of certainty, whose authors knew God and proclaimed this knowledge in no uncertain terms. Hymns analysing the psychology of doubt might help some, but held no appeal for me. It was therefore natural that I should fall for 'Great God of wonders' (38 H. & P.). Here was an author whose faith was firmly based on a God who pardons freely just because He is the Father of our Lord and Saviour Jesus Christ, the ultimate revelation of His love. But who was this man, Samuel Davies (1723-61), who wrote these confident words? Almost contemporary with the Wesleys he was an American Presbyterian minister, who made the hazardous journey to England on behalf of the New Jersey Presbyterian College on a fund-raising trip, the Principal of the College being the famous Jonathan Edwards, pioneer of the 'Great Awakening'. Later Samuel succeeded Edwards in that position, but regrettably he died at the age of 38; to how many students, I wonder, did he impart his rock-like faith in those few years?

I must confess that I liked this hymn because, when our little choir was at full strength and there were at least two good basses (plus me), we would sing it to Newton's 'Sovereignty', a tune which had been safely put out of harm's way in the Appendix of the 1904 book. My voice had broken by then and I was a budding bass, but standing between my more experienced friends I was swept along in the rolling harmonies of that refrain.

It has often been said that the eighteenth century was so overshadowed by the genius of Charles Wesley that no other notable authors emerged then. It is true that no one at that time produced hymns at such a rate or of such quality as he did, but there were several other notable authors roughly contemporary with him: we have just been looking at one - admittedly American - but other names spring to mind. *JOHN CENNICK* is now reduced to only one hymn, his lovely 'Ere I sleep' (638 H. & P.). I remember loving to sing his 'Thou great Redeemer, dying Lamb', with the last verse where Jesus is described as 'Thou great Melchisedek' - are we now not knowledgeable enough to know what this means?

ROBERT ROBINSON

The same question might be asked about another hymn of that period: 'Come, thou fount of every blessing' (517 H. & P.), where the reference to 'raising my Ebenezer' in verse 2 has been obliterated: is this an improvement? I admit the rhyme is better now, but do we have to remove every reference that makes us think for ourselves? In any case, look up 1 Samuel 7: v.12 and you will see what it means.

The writer, Robert Robinson (1735-90), was a bright young spark who thought he could make a fool of George Whitfield (of all people). In his own words he came "to scoff at those poor deluded Methodists, but I came away envying their happiness". In fact it made him miserable, but it was the start of a three year process towards full Christian faith. Robert's mother had been widowed when he was young and had had a struggle to bring up her family; she could not control the lively and rebellious Robert, although she was a Christian woman and would have liked her son to become a clergyman. His changing lifestyle must have been a comfort to her. He was now aged twenty and attended Methodist services regularly, even hearing John Wesley preach several times. Meanwhile he began taking occasional services and quickly developed an impressive oratorical style. He 'filled a gap' at a Mildenhall chapel a few times and they were so overwhelmed by this gifted young man that they pressed him to take on pastoral charge. Many testified to his fine voice, power of expression and intonation, which he could use to sway a congregation, it seemed, at will. Within a year he was invited to and accepted the pastorate of an Independent Chapel in Norwich, his home town.

Later he again changed direction, moving to Cambridge to become minister of the Baptist Chapel there (after receiving adult baptism to make him eligible to be instituted as pastor). Strange as it may seem, all this was done without any formal training or ordination, which goes to show his contempt for any authority except his own, and his unreliability. In spite of this, his amazing capacity for self education made him acceptable to churches, even large ones who would take him on his merits. He began writing a book 'A plea for the divinity of our Lord' which was hailed as a model of theological logic by Christians of all denominations and on the strength of this book many pressed him to train for ordination in the Church of England. Predictably he turned down the suggestion.

That he was a man of great stamina is obvious: in addition to his Sunday services he accepted preaching appointments anywhere within reach during the week and, like Paul, he strove to be self sufficient, running his own farm and corn business which he had set up in his youth. Just how long he managed to keep up this double life we do not know, but it seems that his happy state deteriorated after middle life. He began to lapse into periods of spiritual darkness and depression - even moral lapses which brought him great discredit. One cannot help feeling that if Robert had allowed himself to continue to be under John Wesley's iron discipline he would not, in the words of his well-known hymn, have been so 'prone to wander, Lord, I feel it, prone to leave the God I love'.

This seems to be a valid self-assessment, for the story is told of someone travelling with him in a coach who told him, having no idea who he was, how a certain hymn had helped her and she would have liked to meet the man who wrote it. She then recited 'Come, Thou fount of every blessing', whereupon Robert burst into tears, saying he was that unhappy man and would give anything to feel once again the happiness he had then. Those were his happy days when he was still young, but probably still relying on his own overflowing strength and energy. He is still thinking of the days when 'Jesus sought me when a stranger, wandering from the fold of God', but in later life he was able to rejoice in the great Shepherd of the sheep who would 'leave the ninety and nine and go looking for the one lost sheep'.

JOHN BAKEWELL

Yet another writer of the same time, who is also remembered by one good hymn, is John Bakewell (1721-1819), whose hymn 'Hail, thou once despised Jesus' (222 H. & P.) is a classic. In no way like Robinson's hymn which is subjective - 'I', 'ME', and 'MY' predominating - this one looks to Jesus, a glorious celebration of His redeeming work and His exaltation to the Father's side in glory. Unfortunately we do not know exactly how much of it Bakewell wrote: it was copied, added to and altered, even in his lifetime and later, so we cannot be sure. Some think he wrote only the first two verses, and indeed these could constitute a complete hymn, but many think the first half of the last two verses are also his, the rest of it being added by Martin Madan or Toplady (both notorious 'improvers').

Of John Bakewell's early life we know little. He seems, unlike Robinson, to have had a settled family life and a good education in his home village of Brailsford, Derbyshire. He seems to have become a convinced Christian while quite young, and began preaching locally. By some means he came under John Wesley's influence and training, for at the age of 28 he became one of his ministers. Again his life becomes sketchy until he was appointed head of Greenwich Royal Park Academy. Eventually he resigned this position - a sign that he was financially independent - and held himself available to Wesley for ministerial duties anywhere where sickness or death had left a vacancy. So he laboured on happily into old age, finally dying at the great age of 98. In his travels in this peripatetic capacity he often came across cases of hardship, both personal or in connection with churches, and any genuine case would evoke a liberal response from his own means. How good it is when a man of wealth regards it in this way as a trust from God.

Wesley included John Bakewell's hymn in each of his collections, but after his death, in a revision, it was omitted - we hope by an oversight. The writer's family were angry at the supposed slight on such a valiant old soldier, but he would not hear of them doing anything about it, simply saying, "Well, well, perhaps they thought it was not worth including". Since that time it has never been forgotten.

John's granddaughter's husband knew him well, knew his habits and his good works, and declared "he was one of the most humble, eminent and pious men I ever knew." When he died he had the honour of being buried near his spiritual mentor, John Wesley. The inscription on his tombstone reads: "He adorned the doctrine of God our Saviour eighty years, and preached His glorious gospel about seventy years".

Chapter 6

EARLY INTEREST IN GERMAN HYMNS AND TRANSLATIONS

I have written elsewhere about 'The German Connection'; but Germany has been such a major factor in hymnology that there is still vast, unexplored territory.

It may seem strange that I should include this subject while still in the section on my youth, but time was passing and I was roped in to various jobs in the Church in spite of my extreme youth - all very fulfilling - but a new feeling was developing. This was pushed aside a few times until it became a conviction that I ought to communicate my faith more explicitly. Doubts about my fitness and fears that I was pushing myself forward went on but finally I offered myself and was accepted 'on trial' as a Local Preacher, so my contact with hymns was a dual one, singing them and choosing them to fit my rather raw sermons. I found a number of hymns that had a certain appeal, but I didn't know why; there were no authors' names printed under the words, so without looking them up in the index I was not to realise that they were translations from the German. Even then, I did not know that they were all written by a group who were called, rather derisively, Pietists. Pietism was a movement begun in the seventeenth century by a Lutheran pastor named Philip Spener. He felt the Church had lost the personal faith, the awareness of God's presence in the individual believer's heart, and placed too much emphasis on externals - forms and creeds - so that worship had become cold and formal. He wrote a very influential book entitled 'Pia Desideria' (Holy Desires) and began to hold small meetings for prayer, Bible study and sharing spiritual experience. These were not to replace regular services in the Churches but to make them more warm and meaningful. He achieved his object, and many other pastors all over Germany caught on to these methods with the help of his book and new life surged into the churches. Sadly, not all welcomed this new inrush of life, while on the other side some were swept away and formed their own splinter groups, some of whom we shall meet later. How strangely history was to repeat itself later on in England!

Spener did not write any hymns, but his movement inspired many who followed him to do so. One of these was *PAUL GERHARDT*, possibly the greatest German hymn writer. Another was his godson, *Count VON ZINZENDORF*; it was through him that the movement spread to the Moravian Church and via some of their members to John Wesley. It was through meeting them while crossing the Atlantic and feeling their living faith, that he was awakened to the possibilities of a vital Christian life, which culminated in the spiritual experience in Aldersgate Street. It is significant that he was the man to translate their hymns into English, having witnessed their calm faith on that voyage. He obtained one of their hymn books and was so impressed by the spiritual nature of the hymns that he began translating them straightaway and actually used them in Charlestown long before he or his brother had experienced their conversion, and before Charles had written a single hymn.

ERNST LANGE

A hymn which impressed me at an early age was:

> 'O God, Thou bottomless abyss,
> Thee to perfection who can know?
> O height immense! No words are found
> Thy countless attributes to show.'   (54 H. & P.)

This now reads 'O God, thy being who can sound?', which seems (to me) tinkering with the original: we lose the contrast between the 'bottomless abyss' and the 'height immense' in line 3. Whether you agree with me is immaterial; in either form it is a wonderful conception, an attempt to describe the indescribable, the greatness of God. There is a resemblance to the hymn 'Lord of all being, throned afar', for this too, after filling us with awe at the contemplation of the Godhead, goes to the deepest need of mere mortals:

> 'O plunge me in Thy mercy's sea'.

The author, Ernst Lange (1650-1727) was born in Danzig, now Gdansk, in Poland at a time when that land was in a troubled state. His father was in the legal profession and Ernst followed him and became a highly respected judge, as such being involved in the political upheavals of the time. In the midst of all these troubles plague broke out, but he was spared; in thankfulness he wrote a hymn for each year of his life - sixty - as a thank-offering for his deliverance. This is one of them, and it has been called the masterpiece of sacred poetry.

I still wonder that such a profound hymn made such an impression on me at such an early age: you never know what children think.

JOACHIM LANGE

Another hymn for which I developed a great affection at an early age is 'O God, what offering shall I give?' (801 H. & P.), oddly enough by an author with the same surname, Joachim Lange (1640-1744), but no connection with the previous man. This is a warm-hearted hymn, very much in the spirit of Pietist devotion. It was intended to be sung in the morning as an act of consecration for the day, but by omitting the original first verse it becomes a general hymn of dedication. Look at the answer to the question asked at the beginning, 'What shall I give . . ?:-

'My spirit, soul and flesh receive,
A holy, living sacrifice:
Small as it is, 'tis all my store,
More shouldst Thou have if I had more'.

I will go on to quote the beginning of each verse, to show what appealed to me. Even before I could honestly call myself a Christian these great words must have helped to prepare me for that great step:

'Now, O my God, thou hast my soul
No longer mine, but thine I am'.

'Thou hast my flesh, thy hallowed shrine,
Devoted solely to Thy will'.

Then the prayers:

'Send down thy likeness from above'.

and: 'Lord, arm me with thy Spirit's might'.

The two hymns, by Ernst Lange and Joachim Lange, are both John Wesley translations: I wonder to what extent they helped him too, when he was 'not far from the Kingdom of God'?

Joachim Lange was the son of a councillor in the town of Gardelegen in the Altmark, Germany. Firstly he trained as a teacher and then felt the call to enter the ministry, holding the pastorate of a Berlin church, but his great gifts enabled him to obtain the post of Professor of Theology at Halle. He is said to have written over a hundred books, mostly theological and devotional, including a widely used seven volume commentary on the Bible. His championship of Pietist views brought him into conflict with those who felt that this sort of thing was not quite respectable; but he was not a man who courted controversy and the sincerity of his faith that breathes through this fine hymn kept him out of real trouble.

JOACHIM NEANDER

How different these Pietists were. The variety could hardly have been greater. Ernst Lange, following in his father's footsteps, involved in the political tensions of his time. Joachim Lange, branching out of his family background, rising to eminence in the world of theology. Now Joachim Neander (1650-80) was a typical case of the son of the manse kicking over the traces. His father and grandfather were both Lutheran pastors. Joachim did well at Heidelberg but got in with the 'wrong set', rebelled against his upbringing and lived a fairly riotous life.

He found that a notable Pietist preacher, Pastor Theodore Underenk, was holding special mission services in his Bremen church, so, full of fun, he went along to criticise and possibly to heckle. Somehow things didn't work out the way he had planned. He listened, waiting his opportunity, but as the sermon progressed he was convinced that this man was right - and more, that his message was for him. This was the turning point of his life, and coming into contact with Philip Spener confirmed that direction yet he was always to be a bit of a rebel and an eccentric. He was appointed to be Rector of the Reformed School at Dusseldorf and here he began to hold group meetings and to accept preaching engagements without official permission for either. Like some young converts, he went to extremes in some ways. For instance, he did not go to communion because he thought some who did were not true Christians. His rather off-beat behaviour resulted in his dismissal from the School after only two years.

What happened to this gifted but very impulsive young man during the next few years is a mystery. He was known to be a great lover of nature and he spent long hours in the forests around; in fact there is a cave near the Rhine still called Neander's cave where he is reputed to have passed at least a year. Whatever the truth about this 'back to nature' period, we find his old spiritual director, Pastor Underenk, inviting him to become his lay-assistant at his church, where he was first 'pulled up' in his wild days. Regrettably his health was poor (undermined by exposure?) and he died of consumption the following year.

Although his life was tragically short, he crowded a lot into it: preaching, writing books and hymns, composing and arranging music. Although many of his hymns are in common use in Germany, only two are frequently sung in Britain. Firstly, 'Praise to the Lord, the Almighty, the King of creation' (16 H. & P.), a fine, uninhibited hymn of praise, based mainly on Psalm 103, with references to other Psalms. This is another hymn that has been added to, subtracted from, and altered, at the whim of the compilers of whichever book you sing from. This present version consists of Catherine Winkworth's translation of verses 1, 2 & 5; Rupert Davies's translation of verse 3; and an anonymous English verse, verse 4, which does not correspond to the original. There used to be a verse:

'Praise to the Lord, who when tempests their warfare are raging,
Biddeth them cease, turning their fury to peace . . .'

which seemed very appropriate during the 1939-45 war. I am introducing the hymn here because, although it was not in the 1904 book, we learnt it from leaflets before the later book was published. It seems strange, now everyone knows it, how new the rhythm and metre seemed at that time. The tune is Neander's own composition (or adaptation) and fortunately no-one has thought of composing a 'better' one.

The same cannot be said of Neander's other popular hymn: 'All my hope on God is founded' (63 H. & P.). This is a paraphrase, not a literal translation, by the poet and musician, Robert Bridges, who came across Neander's verses and was so impressed by their dignity and sense of trust in God that he included it in his 'Yattendon Hymnal'. He set it to the tune that Neander had written for it and called it 'Mein Hoffnung', the first words of the German original. Now I have great respect for Herbert Howells, but I can only regret that his tune 'Michael' seems to have replaced the original one, and it seems rather trivial in comparison with the dignity of 'Mein Hoffnung' - but then, not everyone has my tastes! (I hate 'Now thank we all our God' sung to anything but its German chorale).

GERHARD TERSTEEGEN

If you think Neander was eccentric, we come now to an even stranger character, Gerhard Tersteegen (1697-1769) - but don't get the idea that all Pietists were cranks. It is just that these unusual characters have dreamed up such fine hymns; most of them were moderate men who infused new life into the Lutheran and Moravian Churches. Here was a man of delicate health and nervous temperament, who went through an agonising spiritual process during his youth, spending days and nights in prayer and fasting. Light dawned at last, leading him to vow to spend his whole life in the service of God; this involved eating only one meagre meal a day and giving all his spare money to the poor. He was employed in his brother's shop but he wanted to devote more hours to God's work, so he set up his own loom in his cottage, weaving and selling ribbons as before.

After a few years his health broke down and severe depression set in, caused probably by his self-imposed privations. Eventually this passed, his health improved, and he felt deep contrition for what he saw as breaking his promises to God. He then wrote out a new covenant, signing it with his blood! Strict allocation of his time was part of this: work as much as was necessary to live; prayer; and active service, addressing meetings in his home, counselling enquirers, and writing.

His cottage became a meeting place where needy souls could find help with their problems, and fellowship with others who were also seeking guidance. People flocked to hear him and talk with him until he gradually gave up work because it was all so time-consuming. His home became known as 'Pilgrim's Cottage', a spiritual home for many in need. Like Neander before him he was highly critical of the slackness of many Lutherans, so much so that he finally severed his relationship with the Church. In any case he was so committed to his own work that he had no time to support its activities.

His life was a denial of two statements often heard: 'There is no salvation outside the Church' and 'There is no such thing as a solitary Christian'. To him his faith was an intensely personal and solitary thing between himself and God, and he gave his life to infect others with this desire to know within oneself the love of God. Although he had a large following he refused to found or organise a new sect. If his disciples found the Holy Spirit dwelling within them, he left them to worship how and where they wished.

Among the many hymns he wrote there are two which have been fairly widely used in this country. The one most typical of his approach is 'Thou hidden love of God' (544 H. & P.), expressing the desperate need to dwell in God and God in him. The end of the first verse:

'My heart is pained, nor can it be
At rest, till it finds rest in thee'

reflects St. Augustine's famous saying: 'Thou hast made us for Thyself, O Lord, and our hearts are restless until they find rest in Thee". The second verse reveals an attitude of ruthless self-examination, also typical of Pietist devotion and of Tersteegen himself. This is summarised in one line: 'I aim at thee, yet from thee stray' - an echo of Paul's confession to the Romans: "Though the will to do good is there, the ability to effect it is not". The last verse ends with the statement of his aim in life:

'To feel thy power, to hear thy voice,
To know thy love, be all my choice'.

This is another John Wesley translation and it is significant that he wrote this in 1736 - before his dramatic conversion experience - so we can assume that Tersteegen's longings reflected his own feelings at that stage in his life.

Which is the greatest hymn that has ever been written in the whole of Christendom? People's answers vary according to their temperament; and what appeals to one does nothing for someone else. But it is noticeable that several literary men and poets - names like Wendell Holmes, Emerson and others - have placed this comparatively little known hymn as their 'top'.

Tersteegen's other great hymn is 'Gott ist gegenwartig' (I give the original German title because these words have been translated by more than one person). 'God reveals His presence' (31 MHB) is a composite work, not all original, but it has been omitted from H. & P. It was, however, written in the same metre as the original German, so was usually sung to the German tune with the same title ('Gott ist gegenwartig').

WILLIAM TIDD MATSON

I am now making a long chronological jump, for quite recently we were singing a hymn to the above tune, which at first I thought was yet another translation of Tersteegen's hymn, but as we progressed beyond the first verse I realised that it was nothing like the original. It was in fact a hymn on the Holy Trinity, and a very fine one too, but it diverged from the old hymn on to that subject. I refer to 'God is in His temple' (494 H. & P.) by William T. Matson (1833-99), who was also the author of 'Lord, I was blind!' (423 H. & P.), a fine interpretation of the miracles of Jesus.

William Matson was a bright lad, gaining entrance to St. John's College, Cambridge, where we was involved in freedom movements, at the age of twenty being secretary of the European Freedom Committee. His natural enthusiasm found an outlet in these activities, but he began to realise that this was not his deepest need, which he found in Jesus Christ. He worked first with Methodists, but later joined the Congregational Church and was ordained as a minister. I rather suspect the reason for this was the difficulty of getting into the Methodist ministry at that time. There have been many cases like this where Methodists have changed allegiance and found a fulfilling ministry in another Church. However that may be, William had a number of pastorates, mainly in the south of England.

+ + + + +

To get the finest translation of Tersteegen's old hymn we have to turn to good old J. Wesley again; but he did not use the typically German metre, using instead the more common 88.88.88. It runs:

> 'Lo, God is here, let us adore!
> And own how dreadful is this place'.   (531 H. & P.)

Whether 'dreadful' or 'aweful' is used, here we are up against the problem of the meaning of words becoming degraded over the centuries. Both these words have lost their old, fine meaning, but the line is neatly rectified by the new: 'How awe-inspiring is this place'.

Then there is the problem of the selection of verses, for Wesley wrote eight (they seemed to have more stamina then!) In the 1904 book we had five; in the 1933 book one of these was omitted, the one beginning with the striking 'Gladly the toys of earth we leave'. In H. & P. this verse is restored, but substituting the colourless word 'things' for 'toys' - a great loss; while we have lost one of Wesley's best verses:

> 'As flowers their opening leaves display,
> And glad drink in the solar fire;
> So may we catch Thy every ray . . .'

These are minor regrets. It is still, as I have said, the best version. But looking at the tune, why on earth has the venerable tune 'Vater Unser' been scrapped? What a joy to sit at the piano, or better still the organ, and play these majestic harmonies! Originally it was the music of the Lord's Prayer, probably by Luther, hence the German title 'Our Father'. Wesley loved this tune and included it in his 'Foundry Tune Book'.

Thankfully we can still get out our old 1933 book and play it as a voluntary; I've heard it done.

In connection with German hymns in general, it is worth recalling how much they have affected many great men through the ages. Perhaps I have laboured their effect on Wesley simply because through him their influence has spread to many more. But pages could be written on the impact of these hymns on people of all types. I will cite just one example - Dietrich Bonhoeffer, whose imprisonment and eventual execution by the Nazis is well known. What may not be realised is what these hymns of the old Pietists meant to him during that testing time. He was imprisoned without a single book, not even a Bible. This terrible deprivation for a man of his intellect can hardly be imagined, but he consoled himself by recalling passages of the Bible. Also, because rhyme and rhythm help the memory, these well-loved hymns were a constant source of comfort, bringing the very presence of God into his bleak prison cell. I shall return to this great man in the last chapter.

Chapter 7

THE APPEAL OF NEW HYMNS

I have mentioned that a number of new hymns were from time to time introduced by leaflet, and *tunes* that were gaining popularity by being used locally in this way. 'Rachie' (Who is on the Lord's side) was one; and, perhaps rather surprisingly, 'Cwm Rhondda' which is now indivisibly wedded to 'Guide me, O Thou great Jehovah'. "Why, there's never been another tune for it", a Welsh friend declared: how wrong he was! (437 H. & P.).

WILLIAM WILLIAMS

The author was William Williams (1717-1791), almost contemporary with the Wesleys, and of course Howell Harris. John Hughes, the composer of 'Cwm Rhondda', on the other hand, died as recently as 1932. He was a railway worker, who lived at Pontypridd all his life, and an enthusiastic amateur musician and member of Salem Baptist Church where he was a deacon and the precentor. He composed hymns and anthems for his choir, but 'Cwm Rhondda' was written for the 1905 annual Cymanfa Ganu in his home town. It is strange that English hymnals after that date were very slow to appreciate how this tune would 'take over' the hymn. To my knowledge the 1933 Methodist Hymn Book was the first to do so.

Meanwhile, for nearly two centuries what tunes were sung to these words? Certainly 'Rousseau' (MHB A.T.26) was used in its early days. Since then an enormous variety of tunes have been tried. I associate Hopkins's 'St. Raphael' with it, but all seem a little tame compared with 'Cwm Rhondda', whether sung as set in most books or with the tenor and soprano transposed as in some settings.

To return to William Williams (although chronologically out of step), what a joy it is nowadays to have two more of his hymns: 'Ride on,

Jesus' (272 H. & P.) is a marvellous hymn of victory written by William while inspired by the crowds being swayed by the vibrant preaching of Daniel Rowlands, when the progress of the gospel seemed irresistible. There had been an earlier translation 'Onward march, all conquering Jesus', but the present one was made by G. O. Williams as recently as 1967, for the enthronement of the Bishop of Bangor that year.

The question remains, is a hymn written in such high-pressure times as the eighteenth century revival suitable for these more static times? The answer is surely 'Yes', if we have faith that, in spite of any temporary setbacks Jesus is, and will be all-conquering.

The other hymn 'Can I forget bright Eden's grace' (417 H. & P.) is equally dramatic, but on a totally different plane. Here is pictured the loss of 'bright Eden' and its restoration through Christ's victory on Calvary. 'Victory?' you might ask. Yes, the author insists: 'One here has crushed the dragon's might' (the serpent in Eden), 'Two fell' (Adam and Eve), 'but One' (Jesus) fought the dragon on the cross and won. Great stuff! I wondered how many equally striking hymns Williams had written and await translation into English. I questioned a Welsh speaking lady on this point and she produced a Welsh Calvinistic Methodist Hymn Book, in the index of which was a whole column of Williams's hymns.

The tune 'St. John (Welsh)' could be a deterrent to the use of the hymn, but let me commend it to choirmasters as an effective anthem for Passiontide, sung by a well trained choir with a sense of drama.

GEORGE MATHESON

This was a time when, as well as using new hymns and tunes on leaflets, some of us young folk loved to make the pilgrimage to the Birmingham Central Hall for the annual Guild Rally - and what an inspiration these rallies were! At one of them we were introduced to a new hymn 'O Love that wilt not let me go' (685 H. & P.). There, under ideal conditions, this lovely hymn burst on our consciousness and more leaflets were bought. I wonder if any hymn has achieved more instant success; yet I discovered later that it had been written fifty years before and was in Scottish hymnals by 1885; what were the compilers of the 1904 book doing to miss such a gem?

This is another of those hymns which have gathered apocryphal stories around them. I remember more than one preacher introducing the hymn when it was fairly new with a pathetic tale about the author,

George Matheson (1842-1906) being engaged to a girl, he then went blind, and she broke it off because she could not face the prospect of marriage to a blind man. Heartbroken, he turned in his sorrow to the 'Love that wilt not let me go', and so this lovely hymn was born. I was duly impressed with the pathos of the story, but then a Scottish minister lent me a biography of Matheson, and there was nothing in it that would fit this touching story. What George did say about the writing of these words was this: 'I was suffering from extreme mental distress; something had happened to me, known only to myself, and this hymn was the fruit of this suffering".

If it was such a personal matter, ought we to pry into his secret affairs? Certainly we should not jump to conclusions, but we *can* look at the facts: first, this hymn was written when George was forty; he went blind when he was about eighteen, so the broken romance does not seem likely. He never had good sight and constant study made it worse, until he was quite blind at that early age. This brought many problems: "What careers are open to a man with my disability?" He had worshipped at a large Church with an outstanding minister, under whose influence he was led to offer for the ministry - but this was difficult. Louis Braille had invented his wonderful script for the blind about that time, but it was to be years before many books were to become available. George found, however, that as his sight failed his memory developed with amazing accuracy and his capacity for meditation increased. In spite of his disadvantage he went to Glasgow University, graduating D.D. and later LL.D. He was ordained at the age of 24 and was appointed assistant minister at a Glasgow church. After two years there he was inducted to his own Church at Innellan, a pleasant Clydeside resort where wealthy industrialists had built themselves fine houses, a rather select parish of fewer than a thousand inhabitants. George laboured there for eighteen years establishing himself as a great preacher and writer, and a very original thinker. It was there that he wrote this, the most famous of his hymns, when he had been blind for 22 years.

He does not seem to have had any help from Braille, at least until much later, so how did he manage for essential reading, for his weekly sermons, and his constant flow of books? The answer was his younger sister, who read to him and was an efficient secretary, taking down his dictation often several hours a day. Life seemed to work quite smoothly, until someone fell in love with her and proposed marriage. It is difficult not to speculate what mixed feelings surged through her: did she want to remain loyal to George? yet did she feel her youth slipping away and the chance of becoming a wife and possibly a mother? Had he relied on her so long that a close relationship had developed between them that he did not want to see broken? George probably felt the problems devastating, but all these agonising decisions were resolved when he obtained the services of a reliable secretary, and plans for the wedding went ahead.

After the wedding the happy couple left, and later all the guests departed for Glasgow. It was then that George was left alone with his thoughts, in the quiet of the deserted manse . . . This was when the mental distress of which he wrote settled on him. Wisely he did what he would have counselled anyone else to do - turn to God in prayer. As he prayed, these immortal words came into his mind: 'O Love, that wilt not let me go . . .' He said it was all done very rapidly, in a few minutes, as if it had been dictated to him.

He laboured on quietly at Innellan, preaching to good congregations, but during the summer months it was advisable to arrive in good time to get a seat. In fact he became quite a tourist attraction: a holiday at Innellan must include a visit to the Kirk to hear Dr. Matheson preach. Eventually, when he left to become minister of an important Edinburgh Church, landladies complained that takings had gone down since he left! This popularity was in spite of what one visitor described as 'the plain little church with pews that could not have been more uncomfortable if they had been deliberately designed to hurt.' What a tribute to the magnetic power of his preaching.

The ministry in the capital was a grand climax to his career, for here he had the opportunity of influencing countless young people to become committed Christians and grow in the faith.

It is strange that some people must seek a cause for the writing of a well-known hymn. Yet another fable is that Dr. Matheson suffered a temporary but distressing loss of faith and that this hymn was the expression of his return to certainty. Here again the story does not stand up to scrutiny. He did, indeed, undergo such an experience, but it was when he was younger - *at least* ten years before writing these verses. He felt so deeply at the time that he was not fit for the ministry that he offered his resignation to his Presbytery, but he said "to their honour they refused, saying I was young and would change - and I *have* changed". So it seems this story arose by linking something that happened in his twenties with an event when he was forty.

I have hinted that Dr. Matheson wrote a number of hymns, possibly the second best-known being:

'Make me a captive, Lord,
And then I shall be free'.   (714 H. & P.)

This is typical of the love of paradox which he often used to great effect and is thought to have been based on the collect which speaks of 'God, whose service is perfect freedom'. In any case, he was following in Paul's footsteps for he, too, loved these apparent contradictions: 'When I am weak, then am I strong' and many others. Matheson's love of the same device is shown in another hymn we used to sing:

'Father Divine, I come to Thee,
I yield, a captive, to Thy sway,
That love's gold chain may set me free
For all the burden of the day'.   (935 MHB)

THOMAS KELLY

We were fast approaching the date of the 1933 Methodist Hymn Book and already I have hinted at hymns which became popular before that date and gave some introduction to it. There were also authors who had been represented in the old book who we were to find wrote other hymns which ought not to have been left out of any book. Thomas Kelly (1769-1855) is one who occupies this kind of 'bridging' position. His great hymn 'The head that once was crowned with thorns' (209 H. & P.) has always been well known. I can recall occasions when we took part in united choirs for big Good Friday rallies in a large church with a 4-manual organ, about 80 in the choir, and a congregation of nearly 800; the effect of singing this quite ordinary hymn with those forces was overpowering. We have already seen that opinions differ as to which is the greatest of all hymns: some vote for this one, no less an expert than Dr. Erik Routley being one of them. It is a magnificent poem contrasting the total degradation with the final exaltation of our Lord Jesus Christ. But how original is it? I was surprised that John Bunyan had written some lines that commenced with the same thought:

'The head that once was crowned with thorns
Shall now with glory shine'.

Did Kelly know Bunyan's much rougher lines that gave him the idea for his fine hymn, adding the thought of the two crowns, or was it a case of great minds thinking alike?

Now to mention Kelly's hymns which were new in the 1933 book (the actual publication date was December 1933, so I imagine it was not in use until 1934; I think it was in the autumn of that year that we obtained it). The first of these hymns was 'Look, ye saints, the sight is glorious' (201 H. & P.). Published in 1809, he entitled it 'The Second Advent' and based it on the words 'And He shall reign for ever and ever'. This is a glorious paean of praise to the crucified, risen and glorified Saviour, sustained throughout four verses, on much the same lines as his better known hymn previously considered: the Man of Sorrows now crowned King of Kings.

The other hymn new to this book was 'We sing the praise of Him who died' (182 H. & P.) which he headed with Paul's words 'God forbid that I should glory, save in the cross of Christ'. It deals with the impact of the cross on the believer in a really practical way: read it through - that will be better than my talking about it.

I think the hymns quoted illustrate a point that has often been noted about Kelly's writing: his style and his themes did not change much throughout his life, yet he managed to tell the old, old story in new ways. This is remarkable as his working life spanned about 60 years, and he is credited with writing about 600 hymns.

Thomas Kelly's life is worth a good look, being most unconventional. He was the son of a distinguished judge in his native Ireland, received a good education and graduated at Trinity College, Dublin with the intention of qualifying for the bar. After reading the works of some of the evangelical divines of his time his mind became unsettled. He was feeling the call to a life of service for God and hearing John Wesley preach he made up his mind to enter college to train for the Anglican ministry. "If Wesley can evangelise like that and remain in Holy Orders, so can I", was his attitude. Unfortunately things did not work out so smoothly, for before long he was in trouble with his bishop who disliked his style. The position at last became so intolerable that he resigned and began preaching wherever he was accepted. Being a wealthy man, he simply built his own church and ministered there; and having built up a large congregation in Dublin he proceeded to repeat the process in Wexford and in other places where he felt he ought to evangelise.

In spite of this impetuous and unorthodox way of working, it should not be supposed that Kelly simply wanted to hear his own voice, or that his preaching was eccentric. He was, in fact, a sound biblical scholar, writer and editor. From whichever city or town he worked, there was a radical quickening of Christian faith and work, especially social work. His own example in this field inspired others to follow his methods, for

45

he had the will to work and the means to finance his projects. His liberality in the dreadful famine years in Ireland marked him out as one of the foremost philanthropists of his country. There is a famous old story (which if you have already heard, you will pardon me) of an old couple, desperately poor and close to starvation and the old lady wishes for death to end their sufferings but the old man tries to cheer her up: "Hould up, Bridget, bedad", he says, "there's always Misther Kelly to pull us out of the bog afther we have sunk for the last time!"

Finally, I remember a hymn of Kelly's that we used to sing:

'Through the day Thy love has spared us,
Wearied we lie down to rest'.

I should think Thomas Kelly often felt like that, after his days of selfless Christian service.

Chapter 8

INTRODUCING THE 1933 HYMN BOOK

I have called this book 'A HYMN LOVER'S DIARY' and I must be careful not to waste space on facets of my life which have nothing to do with the appreciation of hymnody, but during the years leading up to the publication of the 1933 hymn book there were a series of events which proved to be very relevant to my theme. I have referred to our small choir, led by my older sister who was a versatile person and a very good organist and pianist; she co-opted a young man who was not a great player, but very musical, to conduct, and things went smoothly until she decided to emigrate to Canada to marry a young man with whom she had corresponded for some while. This was a minor crisis, but there was a girl of sixteen, Adelina Wood, who had helped her out a few times and who was now thrown in at the deep end as joint organist. I was impressed by the sensitivity of her playing and many remarked that she had a great future.

What has this to do with the subject of this book? you may well wonder. I think all will be clear, for a few years later our choirmaster also moved away to get married, and though I was never officially appointed I somehow drifted into his place; and Addie, as she was always known, and I had much more to do with one another. We were already friends, but now, although we were very young, we wanted each other's company more and more until we were sure we were to be partners - not only in the common interest of the Church and music, but for life.

This was the position when the new hymn book was acquired for our Church, so as an engaged couple we set about teaching the choir all the riches that we kept on finding in this historic new hymnal. I use that word intentionally, for this was not just a revision but the visible symbol of Methodist Union. The two major streams of the three groups who came together in 1932 each had their own hymnals of which they were justly proud. We belonged to the Wesleyan stream, and the Primitive Methodists were not strong in our area, so there were few of the problems experienced in some districts.

Quite frankly, we found our own hymn book a little 'stuffy' musically, owing to the august influence of the musical editor, Sir Frederick Bridge; and as regards the words, even allowing for their greatness, about 45% by the Wesley brothers was a bit one-sided. So we welcomed the new book with lively anticipation and were not disappointed as we opened it on our music desks and gloried in all the new treasures.

Looking through the book, my eye fell first on *GODFREY THRING*'s old favourite, 'Saviour, blessed Saviour' (274 H. & P.) set to a tune new to me, Coward's 'Norfolk Park', which was inherited from the Primitive Methodist Hymn Book (of 1889) he had helped to revise. The old tune - with memories of Council School days - I was glad to find gone, and sitting down to try the new one, I was immediately captivated by it. I still think it is one of the best hymn tunes ever. *Henry (later Sir Henry) Coward* is one of those cases - of which we shall see others later - of an underprivileged boy who made good. He began his apprenticeship in a Sheffield cutlery factory at the age of nine, as a fatherless boy living in the slums. But one of his workmates, seeing that his heart was not really in his work, told him, "It's them that uses their heads as gets things done". Having to work 12 or 13 hours a day, he got up at 5 am to study books, and especially music. Entirely self-educated, he left the cutlery trade, became a teacher and later a headmaster. He continued to study, passed his Mus.B., and would not rest until he had obtained his Doctorate. Someone then suggested to him that he had reached the top and could relax his efforts, but he rebuffed them, saying that this was not the end but a challenging beginning.

He became the leading choir conductor in northern England, taking his choirs on many foreign tours. He kept up this amazingly active life for 50 years and lived to the great age of 95. When he was able to get away from the Sheffield slums and see the beauties of nature, his eyes were opened to the glory of God's creation; thus a sense of reverence for the Creator grew in him, which was revealed in his music. What a wonderful life, lived to the glory of God through beautiful music!

Turning from the new tune to the familiar words, the striking thing is the similarity in the construction of the opening lines of each verse:

48

'Saviour, blessed Saviour . . .
'Nearer, ever nearer . . .
'Clearer still and clearer . . .'   and so on.

Originally there were nine verses, presumably with processionals in mind, so various selections are made for congregational singing - no easy task, for all the verses are good. The author, Prebendary Thring, could hardly have been more different from the composer, Sir Henry Coward: brought up in the village of Alford, Somerset, where his father was rector, he had all the advantages of a good education in his youth and he had a famous brother, Edward, who did for Uppingham School what Arnold did for Rugby. After ordination he held two curacies, then followed his father in the same living, writing many hymns and compiling a number of hymn collections and publishing several books, until at the age of 53 he became prebendary of Wells Cathedral.

With equal joy I thumped through *SILVESTER HORNE*'s 'For the might of Thine arm we bless Thee' (435 H. & P.), a fine new hymn on the continuity of the Church, reminiscent of Gill's 'We come unto our fathers' God'; and Horne's other hymn, on the Second Advent (one of the best I have come across), 'Sing we the King who is coming to reign'. (244 H. & P.) He wrote these stirring words to fit C. H. Gabriel's tune 'The Glory Song' because he thought the original words "an inadequate statement of the Christian faith". Now we have here a glowing anticipation of the glories of Christ's reign on earth.

WILLIAM YOUNG FULLERTON

A hymn with a similar theme is 'I cannot tell why he, whom angels worship' (238 H. & P.). Each verse begins with the words 'I cannot tell' but halfway through bursts forth with the answer of firm assurance: 'But this I know . . .' The emphasis here is rather more on the triumph of the World Church - each nation's response to Christ. The author, William Young Fullerton, was an Irishman, brought up as a Presbyterian, who came to London and was so deeply influenced by the preaching of the great C. H. Spurgeon that he became a Baptist and trained for the ministry. After his ordination he spent most of his life as assistant minister at Spurgeon's Tabernacle. He later accepted a pastorate in Leicester, but his exceptional gifts led him to travel widely as Home Secretary of the Baptist Missionary Society, then to his election as President of the Baptist Union. He was a man of enormous physique, his relaxation - if you can call it that - being mountaineering. I remember seeing a picture of him in a newspaper, when aged over 70, waiting to board a train on the way to some Church Conference, and a reporter asked him when he hoped to retire and how long he expected to live: pointing to his suitcase he replied: "I've got my bags packed ready to go, but till the train comes in I'll go on working". With this serene faith and ready wit, he went on until the train did come in, at the age of 75.

He wrote his hymn to be sung to the tune 'Londonderry Air' - which can cause a problem with a small congregation - but the words fit it admirably, with the high passages in the tune emphasising the triumphant second half of each verse. Mercifully it is set a third lower in 'Hymns and Psalms'.

JOHN DRYDEN

I had never been very keen on Dryden's translation of the ancient 9th century hymn 'Veni, Creator Spiritu', perhaps because it used to be set to S. S. Wesley's rather laboured tune 'Wrestling Jacob'. Then I found the anthem by *Thomas Attwood,* arranged and lowered to fit it. We were already well acquainted with the original anthem set to Bishop *JOHN COSIN*'s translation of the same Latin poem, 'Come, Holy Ghost, our souls inspire' (283 H. & P.), and it is interesting to compare this with Dryden's version. It will be obvious that Dryden begins at the beginning, while Cosin's hymn says nothing about the 'Creator Spirit' which reflects Genesis 1: v.2: 'The Spirit of God moved over the face of the waters'. Dryden does so with the words:

'Creator Spirit, by whose aid
The World's foundations first were laid'   (285 H. & P.)

Attwood's tune brought this hymn alive for me, for it is a lovely melody with a childlike simplicity, and with a story behind it which is well worth telling. There was to be an ordination service at St. Paul's Cathedral, where Attwood was organist, on Trinity Sunday 1831. Two days before the event the Bishop of London asked him if he could do an anthem with these words on the following Sunday (a typical piece of clerical lack of understanding of the problems of training a choir!). Attwood took up the challenge, threw off this simple setting in a few hours, and (we assume) scribbled out a few copies - with some help, I hope - but with no chance of a rehearsal. But he had his plans. On the Sunday morning he set off from his home in Norwood as was his custom, to drive his faithful pony (I seem to remember her name was Peggy) and trap the five miles or so of country roads into London. On the way he used to pick up one of his best choirboys to give him a lift. The boy (whose name I have forgotten) was waiting at the appointed spot and was surprised to see his boss with his head down, still writing, and the reins hanging loose over the front of the trap. The intelligent pony drew to the side and stopped without the driver's help and the boy climbed in. "Here, learn this", said Attwood, "I want you to sing it this morning"; so with him humming and the boy singing they trotted into the city. The anthem went well and the Bishop was delighted. The boy sang the first verse as a solo, while the rest of the choir learnt the other verses from him - an incredible feat of sight-reading.

THEODORE MONOD

I do not want to devote too much space to hymn tunes, but I feel I must add another to this short list of hymns which have been given a new lease of influence with a change of tune. This is a great area of debate: is the tune as important as the words - or more so? My short answer is that the words are of prime importance, needing to be true and conveying truth in language worthy of that truth; the tune, too, should have that quality - difficult to define - which conveys the truth to the singer. This was so, in my case, with the hymn 'O the bitter shame and sorrow' (538 H. & P.). We used to sing it to a tune which might have been good music for some words, but it killed this simple but impressive hymn. I remember we preferred to sing it to a homespun tune of our own which went down quite well. But when I opened the new book to this page and played *J. Mountain's* 'All of Thee', it seemed just right: simply and melodious, expressing this sincere aspiration to be all like Christ, without any elaboration in the music. James Mountain was a Countess of Huntingdon minister who, though being English, was deeply influenced by methods used by Moody and Sankey in their evangelistic campaigns which assisted them in their work; this tune is in their style. Although not professing to be a musician, he loved music and wrote a few hymns which he included in 'Hymns of Consecration and Faith', which he compiled.

The words of the hymn are by *THEODORE MONOD* (1836-1921), a Frenchman born in Paris, yet trained in an American Seminary, who returned to France as minister of the Reformed Church in Paris. Strangely, this hymn was written in English while he was attending a series of consecration meetings here. He based it on the words of John the Baptist: 'He must increase but I must decrease'.

SAMUEL CROSSMAN

Two older hymns were given a new lease of life by being set to music by modern composers. The first is 'My song is love unknown' (173 H. & P.). This was not completely new, having been set to other music in some previous books, but I had not seen it before and I must confess when I saw it in the new book I was not impressed. Seven verses, to a tune by John Ireland! He had never been my favourite modern composer and when I played the tune over I thought it was a bit angular - but perhaps not so bad. I could not have imagined that this would so completely supplant any other tunes that had been tried. The words appealed to me instantly - I had always been fond of the 17th century poets, and here I thought I recognised a familiar style, that of Baxter, Herbert, Vaughan and others; so I looked at the name and dates: yes, (1624-83), Samuel Crossman: who was he and what other age could produce lines like:

> 'Heaven was His throne;
> But mine the tomb
> Wherein He lay'?

The hymn is a fairly straightforward paraphrase of Christ's passion and death, mainly as told by Matthew, ending with the simple assertion:

> 'This is my Friend,
> In whose sweet praise
> I all my days
> Could gladly spend'.

Unfortunately little is known of Crossman's life. He is thought to have been born in Suffolk, ordained and have held livings in that county and Essex. We assume he was of the Puritan school of thought, and like Baxter and others he found this no obstacle to him serving God as a minister in the Established Church; but these were troubled times and when the restoration came he was ejected from his living, though seems to have been given the choice of being reinstated if he accepted episcopal ordination. We can only guess what lay behind this: he must have been a godly man or this offer would not have been made. He complied with these terms and we assume he thought he could serve God in that capacity best.

52

I cannot believe he was a mere 'Vicar of Bray': surely a time-server of that sort could not have written verses like this: 'My Lord . . .', 'My Friend . . .', 'dear King . . .'. And this hymn was written a few years after his compliance with the reinstatement terms. We know he gained some preferment in the Church: he was Prebendary of Bristol Cathedral until he was elected Dean at the age of 59, but sadly he died within a few weeks of this appointment. Would that we knew more about this saintly man who served God in these troubled times.

BIANCO DA SIENA

The other hymn that was to become popular at this time was 'Come down, O Love divine' (281 H. & P.). But now we are looking at a hymn that was practically unknown until Ralph Vaughan Williams composed the tune 'Down Ampney' for insertion in the English Hymnal, naming it after his birthplace in the Cotswolds, where his father was vicar. This is not the place to go into the life of this great composer except as it affects hymn tunes. He studied under the great Max Bruch in Berlin, but later he became deeply interested in collecting, arranging and harmonising English folk melodies. These he felt were the tunes which should be the music for worship. Here he collaborated with Martin and Geoffrey Shaw, for their attitude was to "throw off the dead hand of Germanic influence" and go back to English music - Purcell and his age. Vaughan Williams, on the other hand, revered the influence of his teacher Bruch too much to throw that off. I feel he achieved a synthesis of the two cultures. He was musical editor of the 'English Hymnal', to the preface of which I would refer the reader. Later, with Martin Shaw, he was joint musical editor of 'Songs of Praise'.

To pass on to the hymn's author, Bianco da Siena. There is a good deal of uncertainty about his early life, we do not know his date of birth, but he is thought to have been employed in the wool trade, but when quite young he joined the Order of Jesuates (not Jesuits - that was much later) and remained in the Order until his death in 1434. This was a rather obscure Order, founded by a saintly layman, John Columbini of Siena, being one of the many movements formed through the centuries to reform the monastic system which, owing to human frailty, was often falling into abuses. Columbini's compassion was aroused by the poverty, degradation and suffering in his city, and his anger was against the clergy who seemed to be doing nothing about it. He inspired a few like-minded helpers who began caring for the sick and poor, while they subjected themselves to rigorous discipline. When plague swept through the city more helpers joined and they found that they even had to bury the dead. Their work so impressed the Pope that he gave them his blessing. Yet the curious fact was that none of them was ever ordained, though they voluntarily followed the rule of St. Augustine.

This self-sacrificing work lasted from the middle of the 14th century until the middle of the 17th, when the movement was dissolved. Why, I wonder? Had this noble Order also fallen from its first ideals? Bianco must have joined when the early fires of enthusiasm were burning and, soon realising the value of sacred song, he wrote many hymns under the title 'Laudi Spirituali' - all in Italian; he was no Latin scholar. These manuscripts were discovered and published in print in 1851, this one 'Descendi Amor Sancte' being No. 35 in that edition. This came into the hands of *Dr. R. F. Littledale*, who set about translating it into the words that have become so popular.

Dr. Littledale was a great scholar, born in Dublin, he graduated brilliantly at Trinity College in that city, was ordained and held only two curacies before resigning. This may have been due to ill health, or perhaps also to the desire to devote his time to scholastic work, for he mastered many languages and devoted much of his time to what he loved doing - translating. He also wrote about 50 books, mainly on religious subjects. He was an extreme High Churchman and it is curious that his best selling book had the rather lengthy title 'Plain reasons against joining the Church of Rome'. Although a controversialist he formed deep and lasting friendships with poets and writers, including that other great translator of ancient hymns, Dr. J. M. Neale.

It is difficult to know how near a translator keeps to his original. Littledale is one whose work is kept as near as possible to the thought of the author, and if the first line of this hymn is anything to go by, it is a faithful English version: 'Descendi, amor sancti' - 'Come down, O Love divine'. Bianco gives us a simple layman's approach to the doctrine of the Holy Spirit that so many find such a mystery. A theologian might have got us bogged down with the mystery of the Holy Trinity while this uncomplicated Christian just cries out 'Come down, O Love divine', so leading us into the truth that the Holy Spirit is no less than Love descending from God who is Love. The hymn proceeds to unfold its riches: this Love burns up, not only our sin, but the passions that lead to sin; it is like a holy vesture which is not put on over a sinful, proud nature, but arises from an inner holiness. Not until the last line does he mention the Holy Spirit, saying that all this is due to His working in the believer's personality. How refreshingly simple! Not trying to define, but just observing the working of the Holy Spirit in one person who is possessed by Him. Much better than trying to start with the Athanasian Creed!

+ + + + +

A distinctive feature of the 1933 book was the introduction of a judicious selection of Sankey type hymns. At one extreme you find some people to whom these hymns are anathema, while at the other extreme there are those who seem to think that unless a hymn has a long, repetitive chorus after every verse, it is not a truly gospel hymn. I come somewhere in the middle. Some of the hymns have sentimental words that make me curl up; some tunes are so banal and the harmonies so bare that they are tedious; and some have choruses that seem to disobey our Lord's injunction to 'use no vain repetitions'. That is why I have used the word 'judicious'. (Some of these have been dropped in 'Hymns & Psalms', replaced by the modern rhythmic hymns, so I will confine my comments to those that have survived the latest 'shake-up').

It is odd that Frederick Bridge, who disliked these hymns, included one which has since been forgotten. I refer to 'Day is dying in the west' (by *MARY LATHBURY*). I can still recall the sense of mystery and reverence that flooded over me as we sang

'Lord of life, beneath the dome
Of the universe Thy home,
Gather us who seek Thy face . . .
For Thou art nigh'.

Then followed: 'Through the glory and the grace
Of the stars that hide Thy face
Our hearts ascend'.

We still have one verse of Mary Lathbury's - the first verse of

'Break Thou the bread of life,
O Lord, to me . . .' (467 H. & P.)

the other verses being added by Alexander Groves.

Mary was the daughter of a Presbyterian lay preacher of Manchester, New Hampshire, who had the joy of having two sons entering the ministry and his daughter, Mary, growing up to become famous as an artist, lecturer and Christian youth leader. She delivered her lectures at the Chautauqua Literary and Scientific Circle. This strange title was the

55

name of a lake on whose shores an annual series of lectures was given in 'Camp Meeting' style. This particular verse was written for the 1880 meeting.

Although Mary was an American she was not directly involved in Moody and Sankey's work. Many authors and composers were, so we shall look at some of them.

ELIZABETH CLEPHANE

Sankey's own tune 'Beneath the Cross of Jesus' (165 H. & P.) was, strangely enough, written to the words of a border Scot, Elizabeth Clephane (1830-69), who was the daughter of the Sheriff Principal of Fife and Kinross, members of the Free Church of Scotland. She was a Christian lady of deeply devotional life and being comfortably placed was financially very generous in all kinds of help to the needy. Not physically strong, and dying at the early age of 39, she filled her short life with good works. When Sankey was missioning in England he came across many local texts that impressed him and set them to music; and quite likely would sing them at the following evening's meeting. This is one example of this practice.

FRANCES VAN ALSTYNE

Most Sankey hymns, however, were all-American. Fanny Crosby - or to give her her married name, Frances van Alstyne (1820-1915) - was a brave little woman, totally blind, yet like George Matheson she had the compensation of a marvellous memory and powers of meditation and concentration. She is credited with having written more hymns than Charles Wesley - some say nearly 8,000. She had a contract with one publisher for three hymns per week!

I have drawn attention to her hymns for children, but her main work was done in co-operation with Sankey. In the 1933 book we were given eight of her hymns. This has now been reduced to two, omitting - in my opinion - the most sensitive and thoughtful ones. Those that have survived are good hymns, but represent only one facet of her style. 'To God be the glory' (463 H. & P.) is a boisterous song of praise celebrating the atonement of Christ. One might not immediately associate this hymn with children but in fact it was first published in a book of hymns for

Sunday Schools, entitled 'Brightest and Best'. But it was later popularised in the Moody and Sankey meetings. The music is by *W. H. Doane*, a very successful amateur composer who collaborated with Sankey in his meetings.

Fanny Crosby's other hymn, 'Blessed assurance, Jesus is mine' (668 H. & P.), is also one of her lively hymns. Oddly enough, this was written to fit the tune that had already been written by *Mrs. Knapp*. She wrote many tunes to words submitted to her, but this tune occurred to her without the inspiration of any words; she sent it to her friend Fanny, who then wrote these words of Christian assurance which have spread worldwide. Both these ladies were Methodists and well provided for and like many in this class they were very generous to philanthropic causes, also devoting time, talent and financial help to Sankey's campaigns which otherwise could not have been as widespread as they were.

JOHN HENRY SAMMIS

Another hymn popularised at this time is 'When we walk with the Lord' (687 H. & P.). Here we have a very simple yet complete formula for following Jesus Christ: 'Trust and obey'. It was these words that gave the author, Rev. J. H. Sammis (1846-1919) the inspiration for the hymn. The circumstances were unusual. Daniel Towner, director of music at the Moody Bible Institute, was at a testimony meeting where a young man was feeling the aimlessness of his life and seeking a firm faith in Jesus Christ, when he said: "I am not sure, but I am going to trust and obey". Mr. Towner assured him that he was on the right road and later, writing to Mr. Sammis, he retailed the incident. Those two words, 'Trust - Obey', stuck in his mind; he sat down and quickly wrote the well-known words of the chorus, 'Trust and obey'. Later on he wrote the whole hymn, ending each verse with the words 'Trust and obey'.

Mr. Sammis was a businessman who, on becoming a Christian, felt he should take some full-time job where he could express his faith more fully, and the opportunity came along for a full-time worker in the Y.M.C.A. He was not entirely satisfied with this, and his unsettled feeling led him to offer himself for the ministry of his Church - the Presbyterian Church. After several posts he ended his career as a lecturer at the Los Angeles Bible Institute. The words were returned to Mr. Towner who wrote the well-known, but I think rather plodding tune always associated with it.

KATHERINE HANKEY

Mr. W. H. Doane, referred to under Frances van Alstyne, set many chorus hymns to music, but he did not always treat other people's poems with respect. A glaring example of this is the hymn 'Tell me the old, old story' (232 H. & P.) by Katherine Hankey (1834-1911). Katherine wrote these words when she was convalescent after a very serious illness, from which recovery was disappointingly slow; pain and weakness persisted, and this couplet is just how one could feel, isn't it?

'For I am weak, and weary,
And helpless, and defiled'.

The poem is a long one, with 4-line verses which Katherine wished to remain in that form when it was published. She was very displeased when she discovered that some transatlantic gentleman had selected some of her verses, put two together to make an 8-line verse, added a chorus of his own and composed music for it which she did not like - without so much as 'by your leave'. It is not recorded whether, although upset at the time, she was gratified eventually that Mr. Doane's setting made her words more widely known. Incidentally, very few choirs and congregations sing the tune as Mr. Doane wrote it: in the fifth line the sixth (penultimate) syllable is often dragged out to twice its length; don't do it, it sounds much better played and sung correctly!

Katherine's story ends more happily. She made a full recovery at last and was able to resume her Christian work. She and her father, a wealthy London banker, belonged to Clapham Parish Church, the centre of what was derisively called the 'Clapham Sect', a strongly evangelical congregation completely committed to 'low church' practices and, most important, having a consuming passion for charitable work of all sorts. The influence of this movement spread throughout England; Clapham Sect congregations were everywhere.

Thus, as strength returned, we find Katherine concentrating on the work she had started before she was ill - running Bible classes for girls who worked in the big stores around her home. Her influence was so great that some of these girls - now grown women - attended her funeral. It was noticeable that as she grew older she tended to appeal to older women and she had the satisfaction of seeing a large number become earnest Christians like herself and throw themselves into the kind of good works that she loved. Her life took a new turn when she heard from a brother in South Africa that he was ill in a remote area where no nursing aid was available; and suddenly she surprised everyone by announcing that she was going to travel there to nurse him. This entailed not only the voyage but a long journey into the interior by ox-cart. All this opened her eyes to the poverty, squalor and suffering that she had never thought could exist, even though used to London slums. Thus was created an added enthusiasm for her:- overseas missions.

Katherine published several volumes, including poems and hymns, which were successful, with the profits going - as one would expect - to charity. What a glorious life for one who could have chosen to live in the lap of luxury!

PRISCILLA OWENS

Our next hymn, which has enjoyed widespread popularity, is again all-American: 'Will your anchor hold?' (689 H. & P.). Many will know of its association with that most worthy movement, the Boys' Brigade, whose badge bears an anchor with the words 'Sure and Steadfast'. The hymn was written by Miss Priscilla Owens (1829-99), one of many she wrote during her life's work as a school teacher in Baltimore, U.S.A. She was a lifelong member of the Methodist Episcopal Church - a fact which shows that Moody and Sankey's work, though undenominational, was really inter-denominational.

I have heard doubt cast on the symbolism: can an anchor hold on a rock? does it not need a softer surface into which it can grip? As a mere land-lubber I am not going to hazard a verdict. The teaching is sound, nevertheless, no doubt based on Paul's dire position in the shipwreck on the journey to Rome, when they threw out four anchors and prayed for daybreak. In verse 3 there is a reference to the anchor within the veil (see Hebrews 6: v.19) - itself a slightly mixed metaphor but with a profound meaning. Incidentally, can you recall other chorus hymns that have nautical symbolism? There are several.

The rousing tune which has helped to popularise this hymn is by *W. J. Kirkpatrick* (1838-1921) whose varied and colourful career merits a pause to consider, especially as his style can vary between this hymn and the simple and beautiful tune to the carol 'Away in a manger' (94 H. & P.). This little tune has beaten off many rivals and reharmonisations and is left in its simple form. It seems incredible that this was not in the old 1904 book. The carol has lovely memories of several occasions when we were able to attend Christmas Day Evensong in Worcester Cathedral. It was their custom at the close of the service for the congregation, which always included a high proportion of young people, to process behind the choir down the long nave to the North Door, gather around the crib by the enormous Christmas tree and sing this simple hymn; the effect in that vast space was almost indescribable - just heavenly, so simply, yet so professionally done.

Now to William Kirkpatrick. He was born in Pennsylvania and was apprenticed as a carpenter. He grew up with music in the family, for his father played both stringed and keyboard instruments, giving him plenty of opportunity to develop his talents in his spare time. When he was 17 the family moved to Philadelphia where he came into contact with some friends who were trying to collect the old camp-meeting songs which were in danger of being forgotten. He published a collection of these which he edited and included some of his own songs under the title 'Devotional Melodies'. When he was 23 the American Civil War broke out, so he joined up and soon became head musician of his regiment, but the war unsettled him, when it was over he turned to furniture making and then to shipbuilding - both jobs allied to his original trade.

He continued composing hymns and gospel songs and as the years went by he collaborated more and more with Ira Sankey, almost until his death at the ripe age of 83. He too was a lifelong member of the Methodist Episcopal Church and acted as musical director in two large churches. Kirkpatrick could be described as a true amateur - a word often implying second-rate, but being derived from the Latin 'amo' (to love) it really means someone who does something because he loves it, not because he expects any remuneration for it. This was true in his case, for he worked at his Lord's trade to earn his living, but music was his love, especially as he saw it being used to God's glory by bringing others into the light of the Gospel.

JOSEPH SCRIVEN

To end this group of 'Sankey type' hymns we will think about another very popular hymn of mixed parentage: 'What a friend we have in Jesus' (559 H. & P.). The well-known tune was by another of Mr. Sankey's musical helpers, *Charles Converse.* Born in Warren, Mass., he received a good education and went to the famous Leipzig Conservatoire to study music. He then returned to America, not to be a professional musician, but strangely he studied law and ran a very successful legal practice in Erie, Penn. He still used music as a relaxation, like others we have seen, composing and editing sacred music.

It is, however, the author of the words, Joseph Medlicott Scriven (1819-86), whose life is of greater interest. Born in Ireland, he was a sensitive man, perhaps a little odd; but he had two shattering experiences, firstly on the eve of his wedding day when his bride-to-be was drowned; then he emigrated to Canada where he met another lady who was a comfort to him, but before they could marry she too died. Poor Joseph was heartbroken and decided that marriage was not for him.

Understandably, he was subject to periods of deep depression, but he was a sincere Christian - a member of the Brethren - and tried to forget his sorrows by devoting his life to good works. He set himself to live strictly by the Sermon on the Mount. He would spend his days seeking out the poor and needy (no social security in those days!) and relieving them out of his own means. In bitter weather he was often known to saw wood for old folk so that they could have a cheerful fire.

He wrote his famous hymn, not for himself, but to comfort his old mother who was ill and depressed at the time. When asked how he wrote it, he replied, "The Lord and I did it together". What a wonderful formula for all Christian work! The simple message of the hymn has been a great help to incalculable numbers: "Take it to the Lord in prayer" - and I number myself among them. But I have some reservations about the last quatrain:-

'Do thy friends despise, forsake thee?
Take it to the Lord in prayer . . .'

I find myself thinking that if my friends despise, forsake me, and I take it to the Lord in prayer, I might hear His voice pointing out the faults in me that were making my friends treat me so: not following my Lord as I should, not showing the 'fruits of the Spirit' - the best testimony I could give.

I am afraid the story of this good and humble man, unlike most of the stories I am telling, has a sad ending. Joseph was found dead in a stream that flowed into a lake, by one of his favourite walks. It is thought that he slipped and stunned himself on the bed of the stream and drowned while still unconscious, though no-one is sure what happened.

I would have thought that no other tune would stand a chance against Converse's simple melody, but because this easy-to-learn melody has been sung to blasphemous words I have heard 'Blaenwern' used instead; and in H. & P. we have a new tune, a pleasant melody 'Manor House' by F. G. Carter, written when he was organist of St. Patrick's Cathedral, Armagh, apparently for the same reason. (Of course, if you do not know the bad words, there is no problem.) I have the same reluctance to sing - and I would never choose - the dreadful tune to Bonar's 'Rejoice and be glad'. I am not sure how far this sort of thing can be avoided and of course a parody is even worse. I cannot restrain a smile when singing S. S. Wesley's 'Aurelia' - 'The Church's one foundation' - if I just happen to think of the poor lads in the 1914 War marching to the words 'We are Fred Carno's army'!

+ + + + +

The 1933 hymn book brought to my notice a number of hymns with a new and different form of expression which puzzled me. On looking them up I found that they were all written by Unitarians, and Americans - all in the 19th century - in fact almost contemporary with the 'Sankey School' which we have just been thinking about. How different in spirit: believing in God, but rejecting the divinity of Jesus, accepting him only as an ethical revolutionary inspired by God and rejecting the doctrine of the Holy Trinity, yet believing that God's spirit was at work in the world. So they preached a 'social gospel', sorely needed at their time. I hasten to add that this is a formula that would not fit all of them; some who called themselves Unitarians wrote, preached and lived well above this bare creed.

Of these, *F. L. Hosmer,* with his hymns 'Go not, my soul, in search of Him' (281 MHB) and 'Thy Kingdom come' (742 MHB), impressed me most, but these have been dropped in H. & P., which I personally regret.

The other two authors who are each represented by one hymn are *SAMUEL JOHNSON* (1822-1882) and *SAMUEL LONGFELLOW* (1819-1892), brother of the more famous poet H. W. Longfellow. These two men were great friends, both tending to move away to 'free thinking' although they were Unitarian ministers. The amazing thing is that, having denied so much of the Christian creed, they had anything positive to preach to their congregations. Yet they did hold them and exerted a great influence. They cooperated in the publication of a book entitled 'Hymns of the Spirit', a title which illustrates their insistence that God is not a remote being but active in men's affairs.

Longfellow's 'Holy Spirit, truth divine' (289 H. & P.), although written by a man who seemed to believe so little, can sincerely be sung by a Christian who believes in the Holy Spirit as preached by Paul, who tells of the fruits of the Spirit when writing to the Galatians. The list in the hymn is not quite the same but very similar: look at the verses - truth, love, power, right, peace and joy. Longfellow, a Harvard graduate, was described as of a gentle, retiring nature, yet fearless to speak out when any moral principle was at stake. He held three pastorates during his life, retired at 67 to write his brother's biography, and so lived quietly until his death at the age of 73.

Samuel Johnson also graduated M. A. at Harvard and entered the Unitarian ministry, but left at the age of 39 to become pastor of his own Independent Free Church at Lynn, Mass., where he remained until he retired. Undoubtedly his charm, modesty, deep spirituality and courageous part in the anti-slavery movement endeared him to his congregation and beyond, compensating for his refusal to 'submit to credal fetters' as he put it. I well remember the impact of his hymn 'City of God' (809 H. & P.) made on me when it was new to me. The first two verses were inspiring enough, presumably founded on St. Augustine's 'City of God' and our Lord's declaration that the Church is founded on a rock; but after that I had reservations as to just what he meant in verse 3 by 'How purely has thy speech come down from man's primeval youth!' Verse 4 restored my confidence a bit, although I thought it could mean almost anything; but the magnificent final verse, based on the houses built on the sand and the rock, swept me along to an enthusiastic conclusion. I was relieved to find other people, more expert that I was, criticising these verses in similar vein: it is a sandwich of doubt and certainty. I remember singing his hymn on a later occasion when the minister had preached a fine sermon on the stability of the Kingdom of God, concluding with this hymn. The congregation sang the last verse so emphatically that he was moved to say, "Please may we sing that last verse again". The effect was tremendous.

Chapter 9

WARTIME LINKS WITH JEWS

It is time I added a note of my personal diary: I left off when Addie and I were engaged, at the time we were beginning work on the 1933 Methodist Hymn Book. I doubt that we thought it would last 50 years, longer than any previous hymn book - a tribute to its all-embracing outlook and style. Our engagement was a long one, for reasons that need not be stated here, but I am sure it developed Christian patience in both of us; but now at last we were looking forward to THE DAY. The marriage service was a never-to-be-forgotten event, with - as you might guess - our favourite hymns which we both sang with all our might. I will mention just one, for it was our prayer for the future: 'O happy home' (366 H. & P.). At that time it was Sarah Findlater's translation of *Karl Spitta's* lovely hymn. (Now we have a new translation by the Australian, Mrs. Thwaites, which it seems is nearer to the German original; but I think we will delay looking at it in detail until our Golden Wedding, when we repeated it in the new version).

This was a memorable year in another respect, for it was quite close to our wedding day that I passed my oral examination (the final one!) and so became a fully accredited Local Preacher - two great steps forward into adult life. I have always found that this simplified life: when asked 'How long have you been a Local Preacher?' 'How long have you been married?' I have only one number to remember to both questions.

Our partnership as organist/choirmaster continued as if nothing had happened, still delving into the new hymn book, changing tunes sometimes (at the most two new tunes in a service is enough for a congregation to take, and anyway we were not always keen on every tune that cropped up) and so time went on. The international scene was looking black and finally war broke out, by which time we had our family of two. I don't remember them asking me, "What did you do in the last war, daddy?" If they had done so the answer would have been "I stayed at home". I had my medical examination, and time dragged on. Finally I discovered that someone who had my future and that of thousands like me in his hands decided that our trade would be more in demand on the home front. So it was that, in between Civil Defence duties, my family life and my church work went on without much interruption, but considerably more hectic.

I had acquired yet another job in the church, that of property steward, and this leads to an interesting encounter. About halfway through the war there was an increasing Jewish population in our area; refugees from the Hitler horrors had been dribbling in before the war started and accelerated as the years went by; and some were befriended by Christian friends. Then came the great influx of American servicemen and with them a surprising number of Jews. I had thought nothing about the pastoral oversight they might have had until our trustees were approached about the possibility of using our school hall for Sabbath services. We agreed that our premises could be used for many worse activities than the reading of the Old Testament and the chanting of Psalms, and so a meeting was arranged between the Rabbi who was to be in charge of this venture and myself. We agreed to keep Saturdays free as far as possible, seating was arranged and a place found for the Ark (quite a utility piece of furniture) and the Sacred Scrolls. Then came the surprise: in polite but firm tones he said, "I see you have pictures on the walls. I must ask that they be removed before we assemble for worship". I suppose I was too astonished to reply, so he continued, "Of course, if that is difficult, we should be quite happy to have them turned round, face to the wall, you realise we cannot have a representation of any living creature in our Synagogue - and this will be our Synagogue each Sabbath". Still a little dazed, I pointed to a print of Reynold's 'Infant Samuel'. "Surely there's no harm in that", I blurted out, "it's Old Testament". He smiled as if he was dealing with a backward child. "That is not the point", he said, "it is still a representation of a living person". I gave up, so each week we turned our pictures round and showed the sometimes untidy backs, quite spoiling the appearance of our neat hall - but that did not seem any barrier to their worship of Almighty God.

I hung around a while to see that everything was as it should be; also I wanted to eavesdrop on the service. Hardly anything was in English, most being chanted by the Rabbi - in Hebrew, I supposed - with the congregation singing responses sometimes. It was all unaccompanied (the offer of the use of the piano was politely turned down and now I knew

65

why - it was unaccompaniable!). I was quite gripped by this strange singing, not unlike plainsong, but wilder and more primitive. Was it the Yigdal, that ancient Jewish confession of faith or was it one of the Psalms? Occasionally the Rabbi's voice seemed to crack and sob with emotion. What was he singing? I did not know, but when his voice did this the congregation's response was more charged with feeling than ever. Were they thinking of their fellow Jews in Germany, relatives perhaps, suffering in concentration camps or being herded into the gas chambers? I found myself speculating what Psalm it might be - Psalm 94? 'O Lord God of vengeance ... Rise up, O Judge of the earth, render the proud as they deserve! O Lord, how long, how long shall the wicked exult? They slay the widow and the fatherless and they say, "The Lord does not see . . ."' The pathos of that congregation crying out to the Lord in their distress has remained with me to this day.

I saw the Rabbi later and asked him if all was well. "Yes", he said, "very well, thank you; but there is just one little thing, could you or the caretaker be at hand to switch on the lights? It was getting a little dark before we finished last time". I suppose I was tired, having been working long hours as often happened then, and I wanted to get home. I shouldn't excuse myself, but I suppose I was a bit peppery, and I muttered, "Look, the switches are there, all labelled, just help yourself when you want to". He gave me another of those 'patient with a backward child' looks: "I don't think you understand, it is not permissible for one of us to do that on the Sabbath - it does constitute work, you see".

I have always thought the Pharisees got rather a bad press, though they were the most forward-looking party of their time, but Jesus was at his most scathing over their insistence on non-essential details like this. It was apparently O.K. for a Gentile to come and do it! I could understand Him, with his deep care for the Kingdom of Heaven and its righteousness, being irritated by this kind of petty observance. I remember once my intolerance surfaced and I said rather testily that these things were quite unimportant and the Christian faith had brought a welcome freedom to all who embraced it. I have hinted at the Rabbi's suave and disarming manner; now he seemed to be wanting me to say more. We had a discussion during which I asked him if he had read the Epistle to the Hebrews. "No", he said gently, "Tell me about it". I had the awful feeling that I had had a few years previously at my oral examination, when a chance remark prompted my examiner to say, "Yes, tell us your opinion on that point". I had to give - as best I could - an impromptu résumé of that Epistle, how it dealt with the Mosaic laws of sacrifice, the function of the High Priest, and so on, and that all this was rendered obsolete, being replaced by the High Priesthood of Jesus Christ; but in any case the whole sacrificial system was abruptly abolished nearly 2,000 years ago, and so on and so forth. Then suddenly I realised that I was rather blatantly proselytising this man, the meekest of all men. I stopped and apologised, hoping that I had not said anything hard about what he held sacred. "No, no", he said. "Thank you for all you have said; I have found it very interesting" - but, I thought, not convincing!

The war was drawing to a close. I had felt our relationship had been one of mutual understanding. The American troops were moving on, then the refugees found permanent accommodation or travelled to get back to Germany and hopefully their loved ones and I saw the Rabbi no more, nor did I have any further contact with Jews; but the memory of those rituals of old remained.

Years later, when television was well established, I noticed a service to be broadcast from a London Liberal Synagogue and made a special effort to listen to it. I had a shock, the difference between this and what I had known! That had obviously been Orthodox Judaism though I had not realised it, but here the Rabbi in all his finery announced the hymn 'Immortal, invisible, God only wise (9 H. & P.)! Imagine my astonishment that Jewish worship should include a hymn by a Scottish divine, *Walter Chalmers Smith* (1824-1908), a scholar of distinction, who became Moderator of the Free Church of Scotland in 1893 - and sung to a Welsh tune! I wonder if they knew they were singing words based closely on Paul's doxology in his first letter to Timothy? After readings from the scriptures, very reverently done, yet another hymn 'Praise my soul, the King of Heaven' (13 H. & P.). I could understand this better, for although by a Christian writer, *Rev. H. F. Lyte* (1793-1847), this was in its full version a paraphrase of Psalm 103 - and after all, we Christians have borrowed, or inherited, the Psalms from the Jews. Need I add that H. F. Lyte was the author of that even better known hymn 'Abide with me' (665 H. & P.), based as it is on the disciples' request to Jesus at Emmaus: "Abide with us . . for the day is far spent", and Paul's triumphant "O death, where is thy sting, O grave, where is thy victory", skilfully drawing a parallel between the close of day and the close of life, which in his case was so near when he wrote it.

With this Jewish service fresh in my mind I got out my hymn book (still the 1933 book) and starting from the beginning tried to decide how many of our hymns would be acceptable to a Liberal Jew. No. 1 was out for a start 'O for a thousand tongues to sing my great Redeemer's praise', glorifying Jesus from start to finish; but from then on I was surprised to find how many hymns were not specifically Christian, many like Lyte's famous hymn being founded on Psalms. This little exercise impressed me as to how much we are indebted to Jewish devotion.

These thoughts turned my attention to a genuine Jewish hymn which was not only new to the 1933 book but was first introduced to British Christians by it: 'Praise to the living God' (56 H. & P.). I have already referred to the Yigdal, the 12th century Jewish Creed, versified later to make it suitable for chanting in synagogue services. It was probably in Yiddish, for it was taken by a German Rabbi, *MAX LANDSBERG* (1845-1928), who emigrated to America and had a long ministry in New York; he thought a good hymn could be made out of it in English. Actually a literal translation of the original creed conveys a great deal more of the mystery and greatness of God and the awe with which the devout Jew would worship Him - something which we Christians must never sacrifice because we have found a new intimacy through Jesus Christ, the God made Man.

I think this hymn still has enough of this element of awe, sometimes missing in our Christian hymns, and accounts for its appeal. It has two curious factors. One is that Max Landsberg had the assistance of a Unitarian minister, *Rev. Newton Mann,* with whom he was friendly, in the translation. This emphasises the fact that both Jews and Unitarians, for different reasons, reject the divinity of Christ, yet both in different ways accept God working in the world through His Spirit. The other strange thing about the hymn is its affinity with *Thomas Olivers'* noble hymn 'The God of Abraham praise', written some two centuries earlier. Olivers based his hymn on the Yigdal too, being familiar with it through his friend 'Leoni', the cantor at the local synagogue. The first three verses are entirely Jewish, in fact it has Old Testament references throughout with Christian figures introduced with them: Jesus Christ the Saviour, His prints of love, the slaughtered Lamb, and even the formula of the Holy Trinity. We now have a selection of five verses (452 H. & P.) but in the 1933 book the whole hymn of 12 verses is divided into three parts, in which one can trace how the imagery of both Testaments is blended. This raises the interesting question - did Landsberg and Mann know this older hymn? I think they must have done, and deliberately set out to 'filter out' the definitely Christian allusions. In doing so they have produced a fine hymn extolling the transcendence of God.

This is true, but I - and I suspect others - when singing these verses, feel the need of a middle verse praising Jesus, the ultimate revelation of God on earth. This is surely the 'aching void' in Judaism, which we pray may be filled. It is worth noting that 'Praise to the living God' is in the same metre as Olivers' hymn and set to the same tune and that the original heading of the hymn was 'A hymn to the God of Abraham, in three parts, adapted to a celebrated Air sung by the priest Signor Leoni at the Jews' synagogue in London'. Leoni (his real name was Meyer Lyon) transcribed the tune about 1770 at Olivers' request, and later Wesley was sufficiently impressed to include it in his 'Sacred Harmony'. Other tunes have been written to this metre, but only 'Leoni' with its fascinating history has survived. Truly a venerable melody, only written down in 1770, but having been passed down orally for generations.

Chapter 10

MORE NEW DISCOVERIES

A popular hymn we welcomed in 1933 was 'In the name of Jesus' - or 'AT the name of Jesus' as it is in H. & P. (74). 'IN' seems to be the original version, but it seems to depend on which version of the Bible you use to quote Paul's great words from Philippians, chapter 2. What amazes me is that this wonderful hymn was missed in the 1904 book, when Hymn A. & M. had printed it in their 1870 edition - perhaps because it had eight verses and was intended as a processional, long enough to take a choir down a very long Cathedral nave. A stirring hymn like this, based on Paul's magnificent words, could be imagined to have been written by an exponent of Muscular Christianity. Not so, for it was written by the spinster daughter of the vicar of Romsey, *CAROLINE NOEL* (1817-1877).

Caroline had been an active worker in the Church when at the age of 35 she was struck down by an illness from which she died at the age of 60. Still more strangely, she did not write these words when she was young and healthy but after enduring five years of affliction; she published it among 'Verses for the sick and lonely'. I cannot help wondering whether, if Caroline had lived a century later, modern medical skill could have restored her to her young, lively self. The wonder of it is that, suffering and restricted as she was, she could write such inspiring words - she must have been young at heart.

While thinking how welcome this hymn was in 1933, I must jump ahead 50 years, when it received an added impetus with the modern tune 'Camberwell'. I have an interest in this tune, for it was written by *Michael Brierley,* a fellow parishioner - although we didn't have much to do with one another, for he was Anglican and I was Methodist and at that time we failed to mix much. He was ordained and married a girl I knew. He became interested in the Twentieth Century Hymn Tune

Movement, started by Geoffrey Beaumont, who wrote many of these rhythmic tunes for well established hymns, to 'ginger them up'. He was followed by many imitators. This movement was ephemeral, doomed to be overtaken by the spate of completely new hymns that was then beginning. Michael Brierley's tune turned out to be much more enduring than most and it no doubt introduced Miss Noel's hymn to a new generation. Michael trained for the priesthood and has held curacies and livings in the Worcester Diocese to the present time.

I have been jumping ahead here, for when we were first introduced to this hymn the tune was 'Evelyns' by *W. H. Monk,* the tune that was composed for it in 1870. Good tune as it is, it seemed to be permanently replaced by 'Camberwell'. Then I was at a recent service where this hymn was chosen and to my surprise the organist struck up 'Evelyns' at a good firm pace and I thought as it progressed "Why did we ever desert this fine tune?" I think there is a time and place for both types of tune.

It is a funny thing how Victoriana is making a comeback. Not long ago Victorian buildings were being knocked down and furniture did not cover the cost of haulage to the salerooms, but now the value of both is being re-discovered and even the buildings are having preservation orders placed on them. In the same way Victorian composers were despised by 'those who knew'. I know of a case of whole sets of anthems and cantatas being turned out and burnt by an up-to-the-minute organist who presumably thought they were "infra dig" for his large choir. I speak with some feeling, for as my wife and I struggled through the vicissitudes of war to keep sacred music going in spite of continual comings and goings, we found ourselves with an unexpectedly large augmented choir when we were going to sing Stainer's 'Crucifixion', or some even more outdated work. This did not seem to present any problem for I called to see an organist friend who was now organist at the church in question and he told me of his predecessor's bonfire - with a good deal of annoyance. So I found myself short of copies.

For these big days - and what wonderful ecumenical occasions they were! - we usually imported soloists, who always seemed genuinely glad to help. On one occasion I aimed high and decided to approach a soprano with a good local reputation, in fact the leading soprano in a semi-professional group who later appeared on television. I approached her with some trepidation but found her both charming and willing to help. Imagine my shock when some years later I heard that she had malignant throat trouble and had to give up singing. She died the next year - a case reminiscent of Kathleen Ferrier. She was by now a local celebrity and her funeral was arranged to be held at the cathedral-like Parish Church. We went in good time and already a good number were there but we found a good seat in the nave; but before long the crowds still arriving were being directed into the transept and worse still into the aisles where the view was obscured by massive Norman pillars. I would estimate there were nearly a thousand present, a great tribute to this gifted but unassuming lady taken away in her prime. I looked at the order of service and noted the hymns 'Jesus, lover of my soul' (528 H. & P.) and 'Love divine, all loves excelling' (267 H. & P.) and found myself wondering what tunes we should be singing to them. The organ voluntary ended and the Vicar welcomed the huge congregation to "a celebration of a beautiful life" and announced the first hymn; would it be 'Hollingside' or 'Aberystwyth'? I hoped the latter, always liking minor tunes, which seemed to go to the heart - in my case at least. It was and the singing was tremendous, for most of the people there were singers and the vicar's words were remembered - this was going to be a celebration, not a mourning, and even the bereaved husband set the tone of the service by joining heartily in the singing.

As I was singing this great hymn my thoughts wandered for a few moments to those who have found fault with it: Mr. Gladstone described it as a number of ideas jumbled up rather than being blended artistically; and even brother John (for this was a Charles Wesley almost at his best) frowned on it - "'Jesus, *lover*' forsooth! I dislike these fondling expressions used for the Deity". In spite of all this I found it reassuring, not at all sad, and when we came to the last line "Rise to all eternity" it gave us all that gentle lift we all needed.

Later came 'Love Divine'; would the organist play Stainer's sweet but rather weak little tune? No, he burst forth with all he'd got with 'Blaenwern' a noble tune fit for noble words. Yes, this service could have been a sad one - with bitter regrets - but no, it was a joyful outburst of divine Love. We sang on to that last verse, first a prayer that God would finish His new creation, making us pure and spotless, but I was quite unprepared for the uplift of those last lines:

> "Changed from glory into glory,
> Till in heaven we take our place,
> Till we cast our crowns before Thee,
> Lost in wonder, love and praise".

I cannot describe my feelings adequately, but since that day, every time I sing these words they have the same effect on me - as if we were being lifted to the very gate of heaven, as we accompanied our dear friend with our prayers. Dear old Charles! - he never had it so good! Could he have imagined, when he dashed off these words which he included in his book with the lengthy title 'Hymns for them that seek and those that have redemption in the blood of Jesus Christ', that they could have such profound effect on a large congregation over 200 years later, turning a tragedy into a triumph?

+ + + + +

BENJAMIN WAUGH

From these heavy-weights we turn to some small-scale hymns that sometimes come as a refreshing change, the first two being by Congregational ministers.

'Now let us see thy beauty, Lord' (534 H. & P.) is a lovely little hymn, to which there was an instant response - a case of love at first sight. True, I did hear some criticism from scholarly types as to what it meant, but it meant a lot to ordinary people. In the Old Testament the idea of the beauty of God occurs several times, which is strange when you think that the Jewish faith stressed the impossibility of picturing the Almighty Lord. Yet in some of the Psalms this thought is stressed, for example; "That will I seek after, that I may dwell in the House of the Lord . . . to behold His beauty and to inquire in His Temple".

As far as I know this is the only hymn that develops this delightful theme. The author, Benjamin Waugh (1839-1908) was an unusual character. As a young man he attended the Congregational Church in Settle and felt the call to be a minister. He trained at theological college at nearby Bolton and held several pastorates before he was appointed to a Church in Greenwich. Here he was appalled by the poverty, degrading social conditions and crime all around his Church. One thing that really roused him to action was the number of boys who appeared to have been abandoned by their parents and were living rough, existing entirely on what they could steal. All the police could do was to arrest them and bring them before the courts. This meant them going to prison where they mixed with older criminals, which simply confirmed them in a life of crime. The Rev. Benjamin Waugh began to attend these courts and tried to influence the boys in prison, when he hit upon the idea of trying to persuade the owners of fishing smacks to try employing some of the boys. Undeterred by failures he persisted until he had seen a few successfully employed and fully trained. The magistrates were impressed and finally referred cases to him instead of imposing prison sentences. Inevitably this work snowballed so much that the time he should have devoted to Church work was being spent on his boys. There was nothing else he could do but resign his pastorate and devote his whole time to this work. Many young men had cause to thank God for Mr. Waugh who opened the way to a career at sea instead of a life of crime.

In his later life his understanding of youth caused him to accept service on the London School Board. Finally he was involved in founding what should never have been needed in a Christian country, the Society for the Prevention of Cruelty to Children. So, we see a lifetime of sacrificial service for the young people of his time, a type most of us would wish to avoid. It was based on a spirit of a man who constantly beheld the beauty of the Lord and inquired in His Temple. God answered those inquiries in a very practical way through Benjamin Waugh.

JOHN HUNTER

The second of the hymns by Congregational ministers was by a man who was not such a colourful character as Waugh, nor did his hymn attain such immediate success, yet I feel sure we should not like to be without it. I refer to John Hunter (1848-1917) and his two-verse hymn 'Dear Master, in whose life I see all I desire but fail to be' (522 H. & P.).

John was born in Aberdeen and brought up spiritually in the Presbyterian Church. There was a time of revival in the City in his boyhood and he was influenced to offer himself for the ministry. He began work as a draper but this call kept coming back and the desire persisted. When he was old enough he offered himself for training, but for some reason he was rebuffed by the Scottish Church, so although discouraged, he approached the Congregationalists and found a welcome. He trained first at their College at Nottingham and later at Spring Hill College, Birmingham.

He entered the ministry with an intense faith but some quite literalist opinions which he came to see were untenable. He accepted that more liberal views did not diminish his zeal at all and at the relatively early age of 23 he was inducted to the pastorate of Salem Chapel, York, where he ministered for eleven fruitful years. He then moved on to Wycliffe Chapel, Hull, but only stayed five years, for a call came for him to return to the country of his birth. He became minister of Trinity Church,

Glasgow, where he really felt he had reached the peak of his career, so rewarding was the work.

Before long he was surprised to receive an invitation to be minister of the Kings Weigh Church in London. It seems that this famous Church was at a low ebb, in a bad state of repair and with a small and discouraged congregation and they hoped that this brilliant young preacher from over the border might inject new life into it. I find this situation almost incredible, for only 30 years earlier Dr. Binney (qv) was filling the Church and everything was on the crest of the wave. Unfortunately these reverses can happen, even in a generation, and at this distance one can only guess where the trouble lay, but it was evidently still there, for he never really fitted in. After three years he had the opportunity to return to his beloved Trinity, Glasgow, and he eagerly took it. Unfortunately his health deteriorated and after nine years he felt bound to retire. He went to live in London and on an improvement in his health he was able to preach once a Sunday for a while; but he was still a sick man and he died at the age of 69.

His hymn, although written during his years of success at Glasgow, displays the humility that often characterises great souls. We have no clue what prompted these words but I feel he must have had Paul's feelings of frustration in mind: "I do not understand myself, for I do not do what I want, but I do the very thing I hate". Paul's struggle was resolved as we know by Christ's deliverance; and John Hunter, also feeling his inadequacy for the task of ministering to his large congregation, cries out,

"Help me, oppressed by things undone,
O thou, whose deeds and dreams were one!"

JOHANN CASPAR LAVATER

It is a fact that all who minister to a congregation - ordained or lay - must feel this sense of unworthiness if they are going to help others. Yet another good man, Johann Casper Lavater (1741-1801), had the same feeling:

"Each day let thy supporting might
My weakness still embrace".

This is a couplet from his hymn 'O Jesus Christ, grow thou in me' (742 H. & P.). We have here not only a humble prayer that only as Christ's strength is the strength of our life are we fit for the work of the Kingdom of God, but also a resolution to start a New Year, for it is headed 'New Year's Day, 1780'.

There is a close affinity to Monod's 'O the bitter shame and sorrow' (qv) which has a more cautious and gradual approach to full control of our being by the Lord Jesus Christ: "None . . some . . more . . and finally all for Jesus".

Lavater was Swiss, son of a Zurich doctor and he does not seem to have travelled far from his birthplace. We do not know what led him to decide to enter college and train for the ministry of the Reformed Church, but he was ordained when he was only 21 years of age. His life was spent in the ministry of two Churches in his home city and his career was distinguished enough to merit an entry in the O.C.E.L., which describes him as a Swiss divine.

Johann never forgot his father's profession and he is reputed as being the originator of Phrenology, the study of the shape of the skull as it relates to character. It was thought that the parts of the brain that gave a person leadership, artistic ability and so on, would show in the shape of the head - so called 'Reading the bumps'. Although largely discredited now, many still believe there is something in it.

I have been re-reading the dreadful exploits of Napoleon, how he waded through blood to achieve his insatiable ambition to dominate the world (like other dictators), but most accounts ignore the fact that his troops occupied little defenceless Switzerland. It was, it seems, insignificant compared with his unstoppable successes elsewhere. English history books understandably magnify the defeats England inflicted on him before his final humiliation in 1812. Where, you might ask, does this faithful little Swiss pastor fit into all this? With immense courage he denounced from the pulpit the occupation and its accompanying atrocities and waged a war of words in print also; he was thrown into prison for his trouble. There was an outcry about this and eventually he was released, but he continued to make his protests. It is difficult to be sure of the details of what happened later. Some say he was told a hard-luck story by a French soldier who, after being helped by him, shot him as he walked away. He was not killed but was so severely wounded that he was completely disabled and died within a year. It does seem that he was literally following his Master's injunction to love his enemy and paid the price with his life.

This incident seems to have endeared him to his people who already respected him as a man who had led many to his Saviour and had built up all in the faith. Jesus Christ had indeed 'grown in him' - not just a good start, but an ongoing process: to quote the end of his hymn:-

"Make this poor self grow less and less,
Be thou my life and aim;
O make me daily, through thy grace,
More meet to bear thy name".

Of *Mrs. Elizabeth Smith* who translated this hymn for us we know very little except that she was the daughter of Professor Allen, of Dartmouth University, and that she married Professor H. B. Smith, of Union Theological Seminary, New York. Mrs. Smith also translated the verses beginning "I greet Thee, who my sure Redeemer art" (391 H. & P.), attributed to the great reformer, John Calvin. (qv) We thank her for both fine hymns.

BERNARD BARTON

It is a strange thing about Quakers that although they do not have singing in their meetings, quite a few of them have written poems that have found their way into most standard hymn books. The outstanding example of this is Whittier, who actually disapproved of singing in worship, yet 'Dear Lord and Father of mankind' is surely in the 'Top Ten'!

A lesser poet, Bernard Barton (1784-1849), was the son of Quaker parents, educated at a Quaker school and followed in their steps all his life. Starting as a shop assistant, he later worked with his brother in a coal and corn business, on the clerical side, then for a while as a private tutor and finally a bank clerk. Here he had a reputation of perfect honesty and punctuality. One housewife joked that she didn't need to look at the clock - she put the potatoes on to boil when Mr. Barton went by!

He married very happily but within a year tragedy struck - his wife died, leaving him with a baby daughter, Lucy. Quite how he coped with this dreadful time we do not know, but perhaps his best known poem 'Walk in the light' gives us a clue. While the first verse follows the familiar Quaker theme - the inner light - the whole hymn breathes his simple trust in God, especially the last verse:

"Walk in the light; and thine shall be
A path, though thorny, bright".

This has been slightly altered in Hymns and Psalms (No. 464), but it is certainly born of bitter experience.

I always say, read the hymn, not just what I say about it and you will see what I mean about this good man's faith.

Although regarded as a very minor poet (he doesn't even have a mention in the Oxford Companion to English Literature) Bernard Barton made many lasting friendships with more outstanding authors, notably Charles Lamb, with whom he loved to walk along the river meadows of his home town, Woodbridge, Suffolk, discussing poetry and literature, and doubtless his Christian faith. Another close friend was Edward Fitzgerald, 25 years his junior, but he found a deep fellow-feeling for this eccentric but gifted young man who was to become famous for his translation of the Rubaiat of Omar Khayyam.

When Bernard felt he might not have much longer to live he asked Fitzgerald to look after Lucy's interests - a promise which he fulfilled only too well, for he married her! It was a foolish thing to do, for they were totally incompatible and they parted after a few months, never to meet again, though they corresponded occasionally quite amicably.

Bernard was a good, conscientious and lovable man, but he would have liked to give up routine work and earn his living as a writer; but no, it had to be a much loved hobby with limited financial returns - until at the age of 55 Sir Robert Peel recommended, and it was agreed, to give him a pension of £100 a year, not a bad sum for that time. From then until his death at 65 he was able to give his full time to writing. He published eight volumes of verse and smaller articles and poems and after his death Lucy published some new works, with a brief memoir.

He was buried in the Quaker burial ground in his beloved Woodbridge. I understand this is still a place of pilgrimage for those who wish to honour this good and gifted man who did not quite 'make it to the top'.

To return to the hymn 'Walk in the light', few hymnals print the original second verse which states most clearly the doctrine of the atonement:

"Walk in the light: and sin abhorred
Shall ne'er defile again;
The blood of Jesus Christ thy Lord
Shall cleanse from every stain".

Chapter 11

SOME FAVOURITE HYMNS FOR THE YOUNG

I have said (in Chapter 1) a good deal about children's hymns when I was a child, but when the 1933 book came out I was grown up, so all through my adult life I have been choosing hymns for children and young people from that book. It had a whole section 'For little children', containing many hymns new to me. A very serious Anglican friend remarked to me shortly after its publication, 'You've a fine hymn book now, one of the best I know; only one thing spoils it, the children's section - it's pathetic!" I couldn't entirely agree with a sweeping statement like that, although I had to admit there was some trivial stuff there; but many of the hymns have survived into H. & P., though they are now scattered aimlessly, it seemed to me, throughout the book. I will content myself with three which have stood the test of time. I should add that they were in use in the Sunday School before 1933 but then became available for Church services.

WALTER MATHAMS

My first choice is 'Jesus, friend of little children' (146 H. & P.), written by Walter John Mathams (1853-1931). It is one of those hymns - although primarily for children - which all can sing, whatever age, for the friendship of Jesus who loves children still goes on all through life.

The author was a Londoner, born in Bermondsey, who seems to have been a restless and adventurous boy who went to sea as soon as he was old enough, and later deserted the sea when he heard of the gold rush in Alaska, taking his place among the fortune hunters. How long he stayed there or how he fared we do not know, but somehow he found the treasure whose value is above gold; - Jesus Christ. It may have been through the influence of the Baptists, for he joined them and the direction of his life was changed. He trained for the ministry, was ordained and appointed minister at Preston, Lancs. It was there that he wrote this hymn, calling it "A child's prayer to Christ".

Later in life he suffered a breakdown in health and, world-wanderer that he was, went to Australia to recuperate for a year. When he returned he was minister at Falkirk, before moving to Birmingham. There was always something unpredictable about him, for in middle life he decided to be re-ordained in the Church of Scotland. Did his stay in Falkirk have something to do with this move?

He served as Chaplain to the Forces, then had a parish in Orkney, and finally he had charge of a Mission Church in Mallaig until he retired, after a life of service for Christ and seeing the world.

His hymn originally had six verses, which is perhaps rather long; MHB printed four, but I can see no justification for the omission in H. & P. of one of the best verses:

"Step by step, O lead me onward,
    Upward into youth;
Wiser, stronger, still becoming
    In Thy truth".

I am especially critical of H. & P. here, for if you have a music copy you will see the vast amount of space wasted - enough to print the whole hymn twice over. I may return to this grouse later, but let me make amends by quoting a hymn that has been greatly improved.

WILLIAM PARKER

'Tell me the stories of Jesus' (153 H. & P.) is a hymn the children loved, with its uncomplicated versification of the actions of Jesus, but I was never happy with the last verse, with its story of the Crucifixion, which we sang in muted tones; then "Sad ones or bright ones, tell them to me". Very difficult to tell a choir how to express that; so top marks for the new conclusion - a joint effort, but mostly by Ruth Fagg, a teacher from Chislehurst - adding a verse on the Resurrection, skilfully dove-tailed in, so that we now have a triumphant conclusion. This made the hymn unduly long, so it was felt that a verse must be omitted; the compilers opted for verse 3 in the old edition, perhaps the weakest one. So now we have a lovely appealing hymn which our young people can enjoy for a long time.

Now to the author of these words: no-one as adventurous and colourful as Walter Mathams, just an insurance man who rose to be manager of his company, William Parker (1845-1929), a man content to be born, live, work and die in Basford, Nottingham. He had another side, however, being a sincere Christian who loved children and worked for them faithfully in the Sunday School of the Baptist Church of which he was a member. Each year new hymns were needed for the Sunday School Anniversary and Mr. Parker could be relied upon to provide them; this was the one for 1885. He also wrote another well known hymn, 'Holy Spirit, hear us' (304 H. & P.) - a good example of how to introduce a difficult doctrine to young minds.

Undoubtedly the popularity of 'Tell me the stories of Jesus' was partially due to the lilting 6/8 tune to which it is set, composed by *Fred Challinor* (1866-1952). He was a remarkable man with a success story comparable with Henry Coward (q.v.) except that he was not knighted. Born in the Potteries, son of a miner, his family was so poor that he started work at a brickworks before he was ten, doing practically a man's work with long hours. This toughened him up so that his father thought he could join him in the mine when he was twelve. Such exploitation of children is unthinkable now - it either toughened or killed, or at least maimed them. Fortunately at the age of fifteen a kind uncle found him a job at a china factory, a product for which the district is famous.

About this time the family was left a piano by another relative and Fred revelled in this new joy, spending hours of his spare time with it. Soon he could afford lessons, then lessons in harmony; and - wonder of wonders - by dint of hard work he gained his A.R.C.M. This was not an end in itself but a step on the long road to his great aim, to be a Doctor of Music. He gained this at the age of 37, but long before that a musical career was assured. He composed many things for children, like this tune, but much more ambitious works - cantatas, operas, orchestral music and much more. In all he published about a thousand works, varying between full-length operas and catchy tunes like this one. Possibly the high point in his career was when Stoke-on-Trent proposed a bicentenary pageant to celebrate their most famous son, Josiah Wedgwood, and the now revered Dr. Challinor was honoured by being asked to write the whole work, words and music. What a life! from pit boy to honoured Doctor of Music.

JAMES THOMAS EAST

Another young people's hymn added to MHB from the Sunday School book was 'Wise men seeking Jesus' (128 H. & P.). Although the title makes it sound like an Epiphany hymn - and the first verse is concerned with the coming of the Wise Men - it soon goes off at an unexpected tangent with the word '*but*' - "if we desire Him, He is close at hand". This is the theme: we do not have to travel to find Christ; He is where we are if only we seek Him. So the author thinks of familiar scenes where he has been conscious of the Holy Presence: quiet lakes, hillsides, cornfields, busy markets and fishermen by the sea. There has been a lot of speculation as to which districts inspired these words, but James East (1860-1937) was a Methodist minister who served in Circuits that were about as widespread as it was possible, from Glasgow to Cornwall, including some urban appointments where such thoughts would hardly be appropriate.

Another widespread story is that Mr. East had saved carefully for something he yearned for, a holiday in the Holy Land, when a dear friend fell sick and only some expensive treatment could save him. He lovingly gave up his dream holiday, spending the money on his friend. He was naturally disappointed, but he came to feel the sacrifice was worth it, for he learned that these experiences of Christ's presence could be found in familiar scenes that he came to love all the more. A lovely story, which we hope is true.

CHARLES EDWARD MUDIE

A hymn for young people, as distinct from children, which made an instant appeal to me was 'Light and life and joy are found In the presence of the Lord' (382 H. & P.). I remember singing this for the first time: the first verse seemed ordinary enough, based apparently on the first chapter of John's Gospel and the tune 'Charterhouse' seemed to match it, but the second verse woke me up with a start:

"Bring to Him life's brightest hours,
He will make them still more bright".

Then the next verse:

"All your questions large and deep,
All the open thoughts of youth,
Bring to Him, and you shall reap
All the harvest of His truth".

"Why, this is for me", I thought, "it fits my case!" I was still young enough for my feelings to vibrate to these words. (Sixty years later I still feel the same; old age still has its questions large and deep.)

Imagine the thrill when I discovered that the author, Charles E. Mudie (1818-90), wrote these words for the coming-of-age of his son; what a wonderful birthday present for a young man! I can remember Mudie's libraries as a going concern, but the improved public library services made them decline and they closed in 1937. Mr. Mudie had a bookshop and stationer's in London and when he was 24 he hit on the idea of charging 1d. for the loan of each book to encourage reading of books by those who could not afford to buy them. He had a good business sense, rightly judging the tastes of readers as to what would prove popular, but barring anything undesirable. He was a deeply committed Christian and would not tolerate anything corrupting. He was also very active outside business hours and an enthusiastic lay preacher in the Congregational Church; he ran a Mission Church in Hampstead almost single-handed and was Director of the London Missionary Society. As if this was not enough for one man to do, he published a book of poems which he called 'Stray Leaves'. How did he find the time to do all this? The answer is that he had a long illness and used the period of enforced idleness, not repining, but producing this book, from which the hymn was taken.

Chapter 12

THE CONTRIBUTION OF 'HYMNS & SONGS'

I could go on for a long time delving into the riches of the 1933
M.H.B. Perhaps you may think I have placed too much emphasis on it,
but let me remind you of two facts: 1. I do not think any hymnal has ever
received so much commendation from outside Methodism. 2. This value
accorded to the book resulted in it lasting 50 years without reams of
leaflets having been used to keep it up to date.

Having said this, news of the publication of a supplement was greeted
with enthusiasm, but its appearance as 'Hymns and Songs' in 1969 was
not received with the joy the publishers expected, some even dubbing it
an expensive failure. I do not think that, but no-one could call it a total
success, for when 'Hymns and Psalms' was published in 1983 nearly half
the hymns and more than half of the supplemental tunes had been
scrapped. This was frustrating for choirs, organists and choir leaders who
had laboured to learn and get their congregations familiar with the new
material, which we naively thought would be in the new book when it
came along.

Having voiced this disappointment which was fairly widely felt, let me
record some of the contents that were a real bonus and were carried into
the new book fourteen years later. I begin with a quick look at a few of
the supplemental tunes. I was personally glad to see dear old J. B.
Dykes's 'Lux Benigna' restored, it's a good old tune and it was the tune
first used to turn the poem 'Lead, kindly Light' into a hymn. Newman
himself attributed his hymn's popularity to this setting. Of course, if you
prefer a setting in the modern style there is also Wm. H. Harris's
'Alberta'. Either is better than poor old 'Sandon'. 'Crimond' was welcome, although we had had Roberton's arrangement on leaflets for some
years and rather preferred it. S. S. Wesley's fine tune 'Hereford' was also
most welcome. I had not been keen on 'Wilton' and there is a lot to be

said for changing to a tune that was becoming almost universally used to 'O Thou who camest from above'. It is not a good thing to be too much out of fashion. Oddly enough, 'Hereford' was not written for Wesley's great hymn, but for a Psalm paraphrase no longer used. 'Lucerna Laudoniae", by David Evans, is a lovely tune giving a new beauty to 'For the beauty of the earth'. I have already expressed what is an unpopular opinion on Herbert Howells's tune 'Michael'. Parry's 'Repton' is fine music to Whittier's 'Dear Lord and Father of mankind', but I still have a sneaking regard for F. C. Maker's 'Rest', partly because I prefer harmony to unison and partly because I remember the expression we used to strive to attain to these lovely words.

ISAAC WATTS

Now to the hymns which 'Hymns & Songs' brought us and which are now in 'Hymns and Psalms'. One feature of these new hymns which immediately caught my attention was that some of them were not new, but old ones which had quite undeservedly been forgotten. The first author whose hymns come under this heading is Isaac Watts (1674-1748). I have no intention of giving even a sketchy biography of this man, who has been called 'the Father of the English hymn' and who has given us a hymn that has been widely placed as the greatest hymn of all time. I have already mentioned a few contenders for this title but I think if a vote was taken, 'When I survey the wondrous Cross' (180 H. & P.) might be top. This was included in his collection 'Hymns and Spiritual Songs' but perhaps more typical of his general style was his later book, 'The Psalms of David Imitated in the Language of the New Testament'. This long title explains Mr. Watts's method; he challenged the sole use of Metrical Psalms which used to be the only 'right way' of praising God and introduced Christian teaching into paraphrases of the Psalms.

We have two hymns from the many Watts wrote, one from each of these books. 'Nature with open volume stands' (174 H. & P.) is a real find, starting from the revelation of God in Nature (a proposition which seems to me to have a lot of holes in it), he goes straight to the greatest revelation of all, Jesus Christ and then on to the ultimate revelation of the love that God has for His erring children - that same Jesus Christ, but now suffering on the Cross.

The other hymn, 'My God, my King, Thy various praise' (12 H. & P.), is one for which I cannot feel the same enthusiasm, even the first line seems in dated language - and I am sure a good start is half the battle. There are good thoughts later, but considering how ruthless was the revision carried out 14 years after 'Hymns & Songs', I am astonished this hymn has survived.

There are also two good hymns, both of which were based on hymns of Watts but altered by William Cameron, a Scottish minister, who made numerous adaptations of others' work for 'Scottish Translations and Paraphrases' (there seemed to be no copyright laws against this sort of thing in the 18th century!) It is difficult at this distance to know to which of these men we can attribute the merits of these hymns. The first is 'Hast thou not known, hast thou not heard' (446 H. & P.); the second 'Behold the amazing gift of love' (666 H. & P.).

PHILIP DODDRIDGE

We turn now to Philip Doddridge (1702-1751), a hymn writer almost of the calibre of Watts and Wesley but nowhere near so prolific. He has been re-discovered in two grand hymns: the first, 'The Saviour, when to heaven he rose' (211 H. & P.), is not so much an Ascension hymn as the title might suggest, but an assertion of the more liberal interpretation of the Apostolic Succession, with a far reaching vision of Christ's ministers in 'the bright succession' spreading the Gospel through the world to 'unborn churches'. A great hymn indeed, but perhaps limited in its use to commissionings, ordinations and celebrations of the fact of our time - The World Church. I find it amazing that it was written by a man living before missionary enterprise had led to the formation of a World Church.

If Doddridge was ahead of his time in that hymn, what about his other revived hymn, 'Jesus, my Lord, how rich thy grace' (147 H. & P.)? This is one of the earliest expressions of the 'social gospel'. It is most forcefully stated:- Jesus is glorified and we can honour Him best by serving the poor and needy for in them we "do it unto Him" - as Matthew so plainly puts it. The last verse must strike our minds and consciences:-

> "Thy face with reverence and with love
> I in Thy poor would see;
> O let me rather beg my bread
> Then hold it back from Thee".

The tune is aptly chosen, Arthur Somervell's 'Chorus Angelorum' is beautiful flowing music which enhances these striking words.

CHARLES WESLEY

It is surprising that, in spite of so many of Charles Wesley's hymns being rejected, some have found a place - some scrapped in earlier collections and a few that do not seem to have appeared since the 18th century. One such is 'All ye that seek the Lord who died' (188 H. & P.), a good Easter hymn (which I have used), which echoes the meeting of Mary with the risen Lord in the Garden, typifying the inquirer's search for Jesus. It goes on to challenge the believer to witness to the glorious fact that 'the Lord is alive'.

An uninhibited song of praise which seemed to disappear in the 18th century is 'Glory, love, and praise, and honour' (35 H. & P.). It is in the unusual metre 8.3.3.6.D., the only other hymn of this metre in H. & P. being the carol 'All my heart this night rejoices' (91 H. & P.). Rev. Francis Westbrook composed a fine, but not too easy tune for it, 'Benifold'. Not a wise choice for a small congregation, but well worth learning.

Just one more of these Wesley reinstatements: 'Jesus, Lord, we look to Thee' (759 H. & P.), a hymn of 'Christian Fellowship'. It was omitted from the 1933 MHB, but there was such a large section with this title, mostly by Wesley, that I doubt if it was missed by many. Still, it's nice to have it back even though it is full of familiar phrases that he used in other Fellowship hymns.

E. H. PLUMTRE

A hymn from a much later age that has become popular in other Churches and which we welcomed into 'Hymns and Songs' was the noble hymn 'Thy hand, O God, has guided Thy Church from age to age' (784 H. & P.). The author, Dean Plumtre, was already known to us by his fine hymn, 'Thine arm, O Lord, in days of old' (397 H. & P.) which applies the healing miracles of Jesus to Christ the Healer today. Why did we not have his more famous hymn in the M.H.B.? After all, it was first published in 1889. With its concluding line of each verse, 'One Church one faith, one Lord', it is an inspiring hymn, especially for big ecumenical gatherings. Part of the hymn's success is undoubtedly due to Basil Harwood's fine tune 'Thornbury'.

GEOFFREY AINGER

From the old to the new: 'Born in the night' (95 H. & P.) is in a totally new style. Words and music are by Geoffrey Ainger, who wrote it for guitar accompaniment, but it has been adapted for piano and organ. The words have a lovely simplicity yet rich suggestiveness: verse 3, for instance, 'You tell us God is good - Prove it is true - Go to your cross of wood'. Later he expresses the hope of Christ's return: 'Walk in our streets again'. The tune with its tied triplets is a perfect match for it.

Geoffrey Ainger is a Methodist minister who has had various appointments leading to his place in the Notting Hill Team Ministry. Although this little gem was written earlier it was included in his 'Songs from Notting Hill' - where he was deeply involved in inter-racial work.

+ + + + +

These are a few numbers that attracted my attention when 'Hymns and Songs' was new, but supplements are not used every Sunday and most of the new items were not known widely until the new 'Hymns and Psalms' was published. At choir practice it was different, each week we would get to know a few new items to test the choir's reaction - would they catch on or not? I have already voiced the disappointment we felt over some hymns we liked being dropped.

I think this the appropriate place to insert another entry from the Hymn Lover's Diary. Every Circuit was given the opportunity to partake in a Circuit Consultation on the contents of the proposed new hymn book - an opportunity which was taken seriously by us. We met each week to consider a preliminary draft of hymns in the 1933 M.H.B. that were proposed to be included in the new book. There were howls of protest at many omissions, so we decided to consider each hymn and vote on it and grade them according to the voting. There was also a public meeting called, which I was asked to chair and a pretty lively affair it was! My job was fairly easy for in most cases of outrage I could report that the committee thought as the protesters did. It was gratifying to find out later that about 85% of our findings had been complied with.

Although the publication of the new book is dated December 1983 there seemed a number of teething troubles and I don't think anyone had a copy until the next year and when they arrived the word copies were so badly finished that our treasurer promptly sent them back. I was concerned with the music edition; I had ordered two copies for ourselves in advance and we were shocked at creased pages and misprints. (We were sent several pages of errata later). The abiding annoyance is the appalling waste of space, I have already complained about this (See under MATHAMS) and the consequent enormous weight and thickness of tune books - and all this for 160 fewer hymns! I even had to enlarge the music desk on our piano before it would stay on!

But enough of the grouses - we have a wonderful new hymn book and we have enjoyed exploring its riches.

Chapter 13

MORE PERSONAL DIARY ENTRIES

Some time before the introduction of 'Hymns and Psalms' we had a great thrill on Addie's attaining 50 years service as organist of our Church. It is true that things had progressed during that period, we had moved into a new Church building and the faithful old reed organ had been superseded by a pipe organ. A big celebration was arranged at which she was presented with a beautiful gold watch and in her own words, "Everybody said the nice things about me that are usually said at your funeral!"

You may recall that prior to the introduction of the 1933 M.H.B., the year before our marriage had been a busy one, learning new hymns and presenting them as 'choir pieces', so acquainting the congregation with them. I am sure this resulted in improved congregational singing, for they could join in with a will when they had listened to something new previously. Now, fifty years later "H. & P. " was published and Addie and I were still at our old jobs (although I had not been at mine continuously), and in our seventies we set about doing what we had done in our twenties - is this a record? The only difference was that we now put over the new material as introits.

We had done this for nearly a year when we began to think of our approaching Golden Wedding date. We both had plans for this. We had not been married in our own Church, which was not licensed for marriages, but in the Circuit Church, so we would have a service of thanksgiving and renewal of vows in the same place. We contacted our best man and bridesmaid and they were able to come; our minister, Rev. Ted Harrison, entered into the joy of the occasion, got out the old marriage register and displayed it for all to see and conducted a memorable service. Coffee was served before the service, for all to come and join us in our thanksgiving and after the service the best man and bridesmaid were photographed under the same arch as we had been 50 years previously.

Why am I saying all this? Mainly to tell you about the hymns we chose, for they were an important part of the service to us. We were determined to repeat 'O happy home' because it was so true, but on looking at the new book we found that a new translation had been made, 'Happy the home that welcomes you, Lord Jesus' (366 H. & P.). This is a German hymn by Karl Spitta, a distinguished Lutheran pastor and teacher. A precocious child, he began writing poetry when he was only eight and continued to do so all his life, but at the age of 24 he experienced a deepening of his spiritual life - Jesus now meant everything to him and from that time onwards all his talents and time must be devoted to Him. He confessed this in a letter to a friend, which could be summed up in Frances Ridley Havergal's hymn 'Take my life' (705 H. & P.) where she says, "Take my voice, and let me sing Always, *only,* for my King". This hymn reflects his home life which was happy because he felt as we did:-

"Happy the home where man and wife together
Are of one mind believing in your love".

We have another of Spitta's hymns:

"O how blest the hour, Lord Jesus,
When we can to thee draw near".   (655 H. & P.)

A good hymn for opening an act of worship. *Here* we see his love for worship in Church, as the other shows his love of home.

We were a little put off by the new translation at first, but on reading it through we liked it just as much as the old one, and it was probably nearer the original. The translation is by *Mrs. H. M. Thwaites,* who was born in Australia of pioneering stock. Her father was an elder at the local Presbyterian Church. She grew up in this atmosphere and was happy to begin teaching in the Sunday School. She gained a place at Melbourne University where she studied French and German - something she was to use in later life. But she was a case of 'wanderer from the fold' and eventually declared herself an agnostic. Coming to England, she came into touch with the Oxford Group Movement, later to become known as Moral Rearmament. This was a movement of the 1920s and 30s mainly in the universities, which had a great appeal to students and intellectuals, and was the means of many of this class turning to Christ. In this company she re-found her faith and committed her life to Christ.

The dreadful days of Hitler's rise to power followed and she came across a Quaker group who were quick to see the threat to Jews and non-Aryan Christians and worked to get them out of Germany to save them from the horrible persecution of the Nazi regime. This was often at great personal risk.

When the war began she met and married Michael Rayner Thwaites, an Australian poet. After the war they returned to Australia and settled in Canberra where they are members of St. John the Baptist Church. Since living there she has translated many German and French hymns into modern English (*not* bringing existing translations up-to-date); in fact she has the reputation of following the originals more closely than some of the earlier authors. Her hymns are popular and widely used in her own country.

(She is also represented in 'Hymns and Psalms' with just one verse of Jacob Schutz's 'Sing praise to God who reigns above' (511 H. & P.). I wonder why only one verse?)

Well, that was one hymn we were going to enjoy. Then we thought of Wesley's 'Thou God of truth and love' (374 H. & P.). Several people had chosen it for their weddings at which Addie had played and although it is a hymn of Christian fellowship it seemed appropriate to use it, both for our fellowship and that of our friends who were present. Imagine my surprise when I discovered Charles Wesley first wrote it as a love poem to Sarah Gwynne - his beloved Sally, as he called her - with only a few words different. Brother John saw these verses and - one presumed - personal romantic sentiments did not mean much to him, or he thought of God's love as being too wide to be confined to two people, whatever his reasons, he altered a word here and there to make it an inclusive expression of love between all within the Christian fellowship.

It occurs to me that this lovely hymn may not be well known outside the Methodist church, so I will quote two passages to show what I mean. John would have approved of this:-

> "Why hast thou cast our lot
> In the same age and place,
> And why together brought
> To see each other's face,
> To join with loving sympathy,
> And mix our friendly souls in thee?"

This could mean either love between a man and a woman, or between members of a congregation. But when Charles wrote to Sarah:-

"And kindly help each other on,
Till *both* receive the starry crown."

he meant what he said: 'till death do us part' - and on into eternity. This was one of the places where I can imagine John turning up his nose and substituting 'all' for 'both'. I wonder what Sarah thought?

We wanted three hymns and without much discussion we settled for Philip Dodridge's 'O God of Bethel' (442 H. & P.). Here we were surprised to find an extra verse after what we had always assumed to be the natural climax of the hymn:

"And at our Father's loved abode
Our souls arrive in peace."

When we really looked at it we realised that the extra verse fitted in with the theme of the hymn and the vow Jacob made of a tithe of his possessions, adding the Christian interpretation - not a tithe, but all, shall be dedicated to God's service:

". . . . not as a tithe alone,
For *all* we have is thine."

The fine tune, 'Salzburg', adapted from the music of Johann Michael Haydn, helped to make the singing of this hymn memorable to us.

Chapter 14

DELVING INTO 'HYMNS AND PSALMS'

As we turn again to 'Hymns and Psalms' I would first like to look at the hymns of three authors which I think represent a bridge between the old and the new. My meaning should become clear as we proceed. Each of the authors had a part to play in the resurgence of hymn writing we have witnessed in the second half of this century.

GEORGE WALLACE BRIGGS

I am thinking firstly of Canon Briggs, of Worcester Cathedral (1875-1959). Please don't dismiss him because of the date of his birth, for he was 25 when this century dawned, but he did not write any hymns until well after this, in fact the last years of his life were the most fruitful in this field. He wrote in traditional metres, but he started the ball rolling by introducing fresh thought and new subject matter. He was a milepost, the last of the old and the first of the new.

As with all these writers I am only looking at a few of their hymns that have impressed me. One of these is 'God has spoken - by his prophets' (64 H. & P.). This looks as though it is going to be a traditional 3-verse Trinitarian hymn in the old style, but go on to verse 2: 'God has spoken - by Christ Jesus' - all very true but it has been said many times and so to verse 3: 'God *is* speaking - by His Spirit'. This is what he has been leading us up to:- God is still active in His world, not ossified in old creeds. The hymn was written in 1952, so you get my point: Canon Briggs was a milepost, a pioneer.

Then we have 'Son of the Lord most high' (152 H. & P.). This goes through the various phases of the life of Jesus, the child, the workman, preacher, healer and suffering Saviour. And all this is summed up in the last verse:

> "O lowly majesty,
> Lofty in lowliness."

Finally I will quote:

> "God, you have given us power to sound
> Depths hitherto unknown."   (345 H. & P.)

This wrestles with the problem of putting man's discoveries to good use instead of bad - constructive, not destructive. This is a theme taken up by later writers, but Canon Briggs was the first to make this kind of declaration, that wisdom must go hand in hand with discovery and invention. I think these few examples are enough to show his forward-looking spirit and remember this was a fine old man writing this sort of message in his eighties.

ALBERT F. BAYLY

The next name I look upon as a link between two ages is Rev. Albert Bayly (1901-1984). Although 26 years younger than Briggs, both lived and were active into their 80s. (Is there a conclusion to be drawn - does the composition of hymns keep one young?)

Let us look at 'Lord, save thy world' (425 H. & P.). Here Mr. Bayly tackles the same problem as George Briggs does in the last hymn. The title is used as the opening line of each verse - with telling effect - until the last verse, which begins "Then save us now, by Jesus' power". The best couplet is, I think, in verse 3:

> "What skill and science slowly gain
> Is soon to evil ends betrayed."

What bothers me is that, although these subjects need our attention, is it natural to want to sing about them?

Two of Mr. Bayly's hymns which we are happy to sing, because they are both on subjects we love, are: 'Lord of the home' (367 H. & P.) and 'Our Father, whose creative love The gift of life bestows' (372 H. & P.). These are on the subject of home and family and should be useful for Mothering Sunday, family services and baptisms, but how many use them? The same question could be asked about 'Praise and thanksgiving' (350 H. & P.), an excellent hymn for Harvest Thanksgiving. It links God's gifts with co-operative labours of mankind and urges the sharing of these gifts with our less fortunate brothers and sisters. The inspiration of this hymn was that lovely old Gaelic melody 'Bunessan', which should ensure its success on any glad occasion.

One more hymn of Albert Bayly's which has deeply impressed me is 'A glorious company we sing' (787 H. & P.), an inspiring hymn for a great ecumenical occasion. It sings of the glorious Church, the faithful, the loving Church, past, present and future. There is the same drive in it as in 'Thy hand, O God, has guided' (784 H. & P.), and with the magnificent tune 'Ladywell' it makes for a moving occasion.

Albert Frederick Bayly was born in Bexhill-on-Sea and trained as a shipwright at Portsmouth, but at the age of 24 he left that profession to train for the Congregational ministry. He ministered in Churches in the north and then in the south of England and most of his hymns were written for special occasions at the Church where he was minister at the time. He began writing in 1945 when the disruption of the war was over and he felt he could settle down to build up his congregations and he later made five collections of hymns for publication. He was honoured for his work both here and in America, yet I have the feeling that his hymns are unjustly neglected, but I hope - and think - that time will prove their worth.

FREDERICK PRATT GREEN

The third author of this trio who seem to me to have much in common, born only two years later than Albert Bayly, is Frederick Pratt Green (1903-   ), a distinguished Methodist minister (hereafter referred to simply as Fred - as he would prefer), yet he seems to belong to a later age. Having little time for much except his work, he found relaxation in writing poetry and a few plays, which gained him a reputation here and across the Atlantic.

It was not until near his retirement that he began to turn his attention seriously to writing hymns. The incentive for this was the preparation of the supplement 'Hymns & Songs'. He had written a few hymns for various occasions up till then, but when released from pastoral and administrative duties he realised what a fruitful area of activity this was for his retirement years. He is still sprightly and active at the time of writing - in his nineties. I have already referred to the longevity of hymn writers, but Fred beats them all.

He acknowledges the influence of Biggs and Bayly, also of Fred Kaan and Brian Wren, all partakers in the renaissance of hymn writing in this second half of the 20th century. All these men are traditional in form yet modern in outlook, they wrote with an organ accompaniment in mind, rather than for guitars or a band. They relied on originality of thought and as we have seen, took account of modern problems and insights. Most were able to be sung to existing metrical tunes.

There are a few of Fred's hymns which do not conform to this general rule and in many cases he wrote words to a tune which he felt would be suitable for worship. A good example of this is 'An Upper Room did our Lord prepare' (594 II. & P.). This beautiful hymn can be used for Holy Communion, but not exclusively so, we recently sang it at a Holy Week meditation and it was indeed very impressive with its reference to the foot-washing on Maundy Thursday. These verses were written with the lovely anonymous melody in mind which he simply calls 'Folksong'. It was a tune collected by the indefatigable Cecil Sharp, who heard an old lady in Somerset sing it to a traditional song beginning 'Down in the meadows the other day . . .''

A good example of Fred working in reverse is the Easter hymn 'After darkness, light' (186 H. & P.), which he wrote without any music to guide him. Here he is at his best, saying so much in so few words - just four short verses in the unusual metre 5.5.5.4. It could be summarised: spring after winter, the entombment, grief and faith, and finally "God will have His way, Welcome, Easter Day: Alleluia." The hymn was printed in the 'Methodist Recorder' with the invitation to submit a tune to suit it. Brian Hoare's tune 'Ridgeway' was chosen. Brian is well known in Methodist Home Mission circles, but who would have thought he could produce such a little gem as this - as original in its way as the words, with its surprising modulation between the last two verses. Having now removed to another area, I am no longer a choirmaster, so what a joy to go back and hear it sung by our old choir and to be able just to listen!

Another unusual hymn with which I have fallen in love, simply by playing it over and singing to myself, is:

"What Adam's disobedience cost,
Let holy scriptures say." (430 H. & P.)

This seems to me to have a carol-like atmosphere and indeed one object of writing these words was to provide something which would be appropriate to follow the reading of the Fall in the Service of 9 Lessons and Carols. Fred also wanted to set words to the tragic Jeremiah Clarke's rather gloomy tune with its unusual five lines. You will find this set to a common metre (4 line) hymn in the old 'Hymns Ancient and Modern' (No. 675: 'The Church of God a Kingdom is') - by repeating the last line. This may well have been Clarke's intention, but Fred wanted to use the full five lines and has produced a powerful effect by 'repeating with a difference' the last two lines, e.g. "And then a judgement day, Each day a judgement day". A shock to bring home the fact that today, *now*, is our judgement day. Again "That Eden is restored; In Jesus is restored." I have never heard this sung and it would not be everyone's choice. Some people would write it off because of its minor tune, but this was what attracted Fred and gave him the idea for these searching words. (Personally, minor music appeals to me, especially when sung to profound or tender words - a case of 'deep calls to deep'.)

'It is God who holds the nations in the hollow of his hand' (404 H. & P.) is another powerful, but more popular, hymn, this time written to fit the music. Walford Davies wrote his tune 'Vision' for Julia Ward Howe's marching hymn 'Mine eyes have seen the glory of the coming of the Lord' (242 H. & P.), as an alternative to 'John Brown's body', but it is eminently suitable for this noble hymn. It was commissioned by the Dean and Chapter of Norwich Cathedral for the Queen's Silver Jubilee in 1977.

The first of Fred's hymns that appealed to me strongly was 'Christ is the world's Light, he and none other' (455 H. & P.), headed 'The uniqueness of Christ'. This is a truth that needs re-stating now, at a time when the influx of other religions into our country could tend to make many think that one religion is as good as another, or that Christianity is good for the English, but Islam is better for the Arab, and so on. Jesus was a Jew, but he *is* the world's Saviour and Lord, not just one of the spiritual teachers of the world. My own recent reading of the Old Testament has confirmed my belief that Jesus is unique - that not only in his teaching but in his supreme revelation of God's love on Calvary, HE is the ultimate Word of God to the world.

Finally, two hymns on aspects of the theme of Harvest: 'For the fruits of his creation' (342 H. & P.) and 'God in his love for us lent us this planet' (343 H. & P.). Both hymns, in different ways, relate harvest with feeding the starving countries, and ending pollution and devastation by war - all causes urgent in our time.

When I published my previous book I had many bouquets for which I was grateful, but a few brickbats, mainly because "I had dismissed Fred with one sentence", while devoting pages to some other authors (who were not even Methodists!). I now apologise - especially to Fred - but I must point out that when my book came out I had not seen a copy of 'Hymns & Psalms', only a provisional typed index sheet of its contents. I had never met Fred and knew little about him. I agree that I tended to write a lot about writers whom I had met or I 'knew' via relatives or friends, who had solid facts for me to record. So now I will try to make amends.

One critic called Fred 'a Twentieth Century equivalent of Charles Wesley'. Now Fred is a humble man and I think he would be the first to deny that.

His parents were poor, for they travelled to Liverpool from their native Shropshire seeking work. They were hard-working Christian folk who managed to start up a small leather-work business. Times were hard, but things began to look up and expand. They had two children and then Fred arrived - a very late comer, for his eldest brother was aged 14 when Fred was born. His father had offered himself as a local preacher, passed through his training and was duly accredited. Later on he resigned because he felt the doctrine of the love of God as revealed in Jesus Christ, which he loved to preach, was not compatible with the doctrine of eternal damnation. I wonder what lack of understanding lay behind this sad event?

The family moved to Wallasey while Fred was young, he attended the Methodist Church there with the family and won a place at the Grammar School. At the age of 14 his parents were able to afford to send him to boarding school, Rydal School, Colwyn Bay. There he came under continued Methodist influence, for the Headmaster was that godly man, Rev. A. J. Costain, who combined the qualities of a keen sportsman and a faithful Christian teacher. Fred later declared, "I was happy there - something that not all old boys can say of their school." Returning home, he worked in his father's business and shared their happy home life - again, in his own words, "a place of piety but never burdensome."

At the Methodist Church he came under the influence of Rev. William Rushby, who recognised this lad's potential and set him on the first step to ordination by suggesting that he should go on trial as a Local Preacher, take his exams and become fully accredited. From there he went on to college and was ordained. He was always grateful that he had these years in the world of business before be trained for the ministry. His first post after ordination was as Chaplain at the newly established Hunmanby Hall boarding school for girls. There he fell in love with Marjorie Dowsett, who was teaching French at the school. (They celebrated their Diamond Wedding in 1991).

Fred's ministry continued in churches and Circuits in various parts of the country, including working in London during the 1939-45 War. He progressed to more important positions until he became minister of one of the largest congregation in England, at the Dome Mission, Brighton.

In 1957 he was elected Chairman of the York and Hull Methodist District, an office which he held for seven years. There, with no local pastorate to serve, he had a huge District to cover as a loved 'Father in God'. He finished his active ministry in the London (Sutton) Circuit and it was toward the end of this period that his new career of hymn writer began.

What a lovely life:- a happy childhood, school days and work in the family business, spiritual growth as a young Local Preacher, training for the ministry, a varied and rewarding ministry, and a fulfilling retirement with the joy of discovering new riches of our hymnody. He is still, as he has always quizzically declared himself, 'a little right of centre'.

+ + + + +

One of the blessings that my long life brings is that I can view the changes in fashion and popularity that take place - yes, even in hymns. Having lived through three successive Methodist hymn books and - as an observer - numerous Anglican and Congregational books too, all sorts of changes have taken place. Apart from new material, some of which I have already noted, some hymns have endured because they have that quality of permanence, so difficult to define, some have persisted with slight changes to cut out archaic language or words that have changed their meaning, and sometimes to modify doctrines that are not considered important. Yet again, some numbers have been there all the time, but have not been in use. In my young days there was a run on Charles Wesley's 'Happy the man that finds the grace' (674 H. & P.). Recently someone chose it, and I hadn't sung it for years. I had linked it with the third chapter of Proverbs and the Old Testament theme that crops up in the 'wisdom' books, and also in the Apocrypha. Perhaps I am now a little more perceptive and I realised how skilfully Charles wove New Testament teaching into the Wisdom idea:-

"Happy beyond description he
Who knows 'The Saviour died for me'."

and finally this marvellous synthesis of Old and New Testaments:-

"He owns, and shall for ever own,
Wisdom, and Christ, and heaven are one."

I find it difficult to imagine how this hymn has survived the feminist assault on so many time-honoured hymns, poems, etc. "Happy the *man*",

"He owns" etc. O dear, tut, tut! I suppose no-one has yet found a word of one syllable to substitute for 'man'. Perhaps by the time another hymn book is compiled, this silly craze will have passed and this hymn will be chosen again by the selection committee.

SAMUEL JOHN STONE

This leads me to another old hymn 'The Church's one foundation' (515 H. & P.), which is so well known that it is in all respectable books, yet has in my experience suffered a temporary eclipse. I had not sung it for years until a recent service. I was then singing it with only a glance at the beginning of each verse, for I knew it so well, it was inscribed on my memory. We arrived at the last verse - another glance at the book and I realised we were going to be robbed of my favourite verse, how I growled out these dramatic words at the Grammar School:-

"Though with a scornful wonder
Men see her sore oppressed,
By schisms rent asunder,
By heresies distressed.
Yet saints their watch are keeping,
Their cry goes up, 'How long?'" and so on.

Now why have they left that out? I mused. Then I thought, "Oh, I suppose they think the Colenso controversy is gone and now forgotten." Yes, so it might be, but those words are wide enough to apply to the situation of the Church at any time and especially now.

At the time of its composition this was the key verse; that was in 1887, and the following year some more verses were added to make it long enough to be used as a processional hymn for the first Lambeth Conference. At the great assemblies in Canterbury Cathedral, St. Paul's and Westminster Abbey, this was sung as the great procession of dignitaries made its way slowly up the long naves of these buildings. Many of those present declared that the effect of the united choirs singing this hymn was so overwhelming that they felt near to collapsing.

The schisms and heresies referred to were the 'modern' critical evaluation of the early books of the Bible, later called the higher criticism, by a certain section of theologians led by Bishop Colenso. I suppose the Hymn Book Committee thought the bishop's conclusions were no longer a threat to the authority of the Bible or the stability of the Church. Yes, the last century of research has removed many of the difficulties which the attentive reader finds in the Bible, and which unbelievers pick on to confuse and embarrass the 'Child in Christ'. As I have already hinted, I wish we still had this verse, even if we mean something different by it.

The author, Samuel John Stone (1839-1900) was a sincere but rigid High Churchman. His father was rector of Whitmore, Staffs, a quiet parish of about 300 inhabitants with an attractive little timber framed Church. While Samuel was still young his father made a surprise move, away from his peaceful surroundings to St. Paul's Haggerston, a poor parish with a run-down church. Meanwhile Samuel was educated at Charterhouse and Pembroke College, Oxford, where he graduated M.A., and was ordained. After a curacy at Windsor he assisted his father at Haggerston, following him as vicar at the age of 36, and finishing his ministry at All Hallows-on-the-Wall.

Stone wrote a series of 12 hymns on the Apostles' Creed, this one being based on 'The Holy Catholic Church, the Communion of Saints', the whole set having the significant title 'Lyra Fidelium'. He took and expanded the words of St. Paul: "For other foundation can no man lay than that is laid, which is Jesus Christ".

JOSIAH CONDER

An author whose hymns have suffered from a strange merry-go-round is Josiah Conder (1784-1855). He lived in a period not noted for new hymns, so I think we can assume that he was an individualist and his writings did not follow any particular fashion, therefore being timeless. He was the son of a bookseller and engraver, to whom he was apprenticed and he took on the business after his father's death.

As a boy he suffered a near-fatal illness, smallpox, as a result of which he lost the sight of one eye, yet at the age of ten he submitted articles in a competition for which he won a medal. Not surprisingly he soon developed a deep love of literature and continued to write prose and poetry, his longest work being a 30 volume work 'The Modern Traveller' which took him on and off 7 years. Unfortunately his obsession for writing made him a poor and unreliable business man.

The family were Congregationalists and Josiah early became an earnest Christian and was soon in demand as a lay preacher in his Church. He was not only a prolific hymn writer but had an exhaustive knowledge of hymnology, leading to his being appointed Editor of the first Congregational Hymn Book in 1836. In addition to all this he owned and edited the 'Eclectic Review' and 'The Patriot'. No wonder he sometimes neglected his business and found himself in financial trouble!

We now have one of his best hymns, 'The Lord is King! Lift up thy voice' (58 H. & P.), a grand declaration of the Kingship of God, which was unaccountably omitted from M.H.B. One that was in that book and has unaccountably been left out of the present one is the lovely Communion hymn, 'Bread of Heaven' (769 MHB). I am sure that in the unduly large number in that section, this two-verse gem ought to have found a place. Canon Ellerton, author of 'The day thou gavest' (648 H. & P.) and many other fine hymns, was pretty scathing about dissenters, yet he said of this hymn: "One would imagine it to have been written by a Franciscan Mystic Theologian". Praise indeed for a nonconformist struggling bookseller!

The other hymn of Mr. Conder's which is new to us is 'Head of the church, our risen Lord' (547 H. & P.), a good hymn for any service for worship not simply for Easter as its title suggests, for every Sunday is a celebration of Christ's rising from the dead - an Easter of joy every week.

PATRICK APPLEFORD

I am now turning to a modern author/composer to whom I must offer the same apologies as I have done before. In fact, looking through my previous book I find there are several living authors like this to whom I gave only a few lines - because of what Dr. Johnson would have said: "Ignorance, madam, pure ignorance". I speak of Canon Patrick Appleford, (1925-   ), born in Croydon, educated at Trinity College, Cambridge, graduated M.A. and after theological college ordained at the age of 28.

Patrick was curate of Poplar when the idea of a more popular style of Church music came to him. A co-founder with Geoffrey Beaumont of the Twentieth Century Church Light Music Group, he became its first secretary. He was a man of many talents, writing both words and music of one of the most popular modern hymns, 'Living Lord' (617 H. & P.). He got the idea from Cliff Richard singing the 'Top of the Pops' song 'Living Doll', and the thought came to him that a song to the praise of Jesus as Living Lord might catch on. This should not be thought of as a trivial song, however, for the use of meaningful repetition of phrases like 'Lord Jesus Christ . . . You are one with us, Mary's Son', 'Born as one of us, Mary's Son' and 'Living Lord', emphasises important truths - Christ human, yet divine. The subject of prayer, Holy Communion, Christ's death and resurrection are all there.

Patrick's gifts have led to various appointments over the years: he went to Africa, where a huge diocese was becoming too big to be manageable, so it was divided and he became Dean of the Cathedral at Lusaka, an office he held for ten years. Since returning to England he has been Diocesan Director of Education at Chelmsford and a Canon of Chelmsford Cathedral. He has also appeared on television in the cause of new music for Christian worship.

JOHN NEWTON

The previous hymn has reminded me that while a pop tune may inspire a hymn, a hymn has occasionally been given pop treatment. One of the most surprising examples of this is 'Amazing Grace' (215 H. & P.), for John Newton (1725-1807) is a younger contemporary of the Wesleys, in fact deeply influenced by them. Can you think of a less likely entry for the 'Top Ten', for the words were - at least the first part - the story of John's life, and a pretty bad life it was.

John had the disadvantage of the death of a godly mother when he was a little boy, and a father away at sea on long voyages. Being worried about his son's behaviour, his father took John abroad with him, but he chose the company of the worst of the crew and as soon as he could break free from his father's care he went to sea on his own. His adventures included a terrifying shipwreck, clinging to a raft for many days. On his epitaph he describes himself "once an infidel and a libertine, servant of slaves in Africa, etc." (I think 'servant' is a euphemism for 'trader', for he was in fact captain of one of the infamous slave-traders with their iniquitous traffic in human lives). I have said enough to show the aptness of his lines:

"Amazing grace (how sweet the sound)
That saved a wretch like me!
I once was lost, but now am found,
Was blind, but now I see."

This truly astonishing change from blindness and lostness to seeing and being found is sometimes represented as sudden and dramatic, but reading his life, I can discern several stages, the point is however, that he *did* arrive. The word 'grace' he used with its specific Christian meaning: 'the love of God for each sinner, totally undeserved' - and to hear this crooned out the way it was seemed little short of blasphemy to me!

John Newton's hymn has almost as chequered a history as he himself had. He wrote it in 1779 for the 'Olney Hymns', at the age of 54, by which time he was vicar of Olney, the wonder of his conversion was still the great feature of his life - that Christ had sought and found such a lost sheep as he was - and a black one too. The hymn never seems to have got into any English books, but seems to have travelled across the Atlantic with some emigrants; and it has been published in various books there ever since. It was in America that it was adopted as a pop song and it was broadcast in this country. Then our hymn book publishers realised what they had been missing. In America someone has added a spurious verse beginning "When we've been there a thousand years", which is unworthy of John's final words:

"I shall possess within the veil
A life of joy and peace."

The story of the tune is just as interesting. It is described as an American folk tune, but it is almost certainly of Scottish origin, so was likely to have been taken across, just as the words were, by colonists in the 18th century. It is in the pentatonic scale, which - having no semitones - has that characteristic sweet and plaintive effect, with only five notes to the octave. This makes sense, as many of the ancient Scottish airs are in this scale.

John Newton was the author of many more hymns including 'Glorious things of thee are spoken' (817 H. & P.) and 'How sweet the name of Jesus sounds' (257 H. & P.), but these are not so autobiographical as the previous one. Two more new to 'Hymns and Songs': 'Great Shepherd of thy people, hear' (490 H. & P.), surprisingly reinstated when so many good hymns on worship in the sanctuary have been thrown out. More surprising was the omission in 1933 of that little gem 'May the grace of Christ our Saviour' (762 H. & P.), now happily restored. It is a simple paraphrase of 'the Grace', Paul's farewell to the Corinthian Christians at the end of his second letter. It is fittingly set to the 17th century chorale melody by Heinrich Albert.

ELEANOR FARJEON

Another hymn which was given pop treatment, but first in our own country, is 'Morning has broken' (635 H. & P.), but thankfully it is now restored to its proper place as a fresh and youthful song of praise. The tune 'Bunessan' is a genuine Scottish air picked up in the Isle of Mull and named after a hamlet there. This is a luscious tune which has the attractiveness of a pentatonic tune - which it is not truly so - but there is only one note that deviates from that scale (try it on the black notes on your piano - key of Gb). Percy Dearmer was attracted to the tune and although it already had words (the carol 'Child in the manger') he felt some more general words might be successful, to be incorporated in his new 'Songs of Praise, 1961', so he invited Eleanor Farjeon (1881-1965) to write words to fit it. 'Morning has broken' was the result.

Eleanor was an unusual character, as different from John Newton as her hymn was from his. Her father was a successful novelist, a rather domineering man, while her mother was a former American actress, pretty and vivacious, a foil for her talented but difficult husband. Eleanor inherited some of these qualities from both parents. Father certainly encouraged his daughter to love literature and to learn the art of writing, but he also completely educated her, with the result that she did not mix with any other children except her three brothers. This made her shy and withdrawn, especially with other girls. She remained so until she met the poet Edward Thomas and his wife. Edward in particular brought her out of her shell and helped to develop her latent talents. She produced books of poems, novels and, most of all, children's stories.

She looked on Edward as her mentor and as time passed she obviously became deeply in love with him. Then came the 1914 War and his death in battle. She moved to a cottage, living on her own in a sort of bohemian life-style, defying convention. All this time there was a spiritual hunger which she did not seem to be able to satisfy. After trying spiritualism, theosophy and other deviations, she began reading St. Augustine, then Ignatius Loyola. Gradually she was convinced that orthodox Christianity as taught by the mainstream Churches was the true road to peace and at the age of 70 she was received into the Roman Catholic Church. She always insisted that hers was not a conversion but a gradual progress of faith.

It was after this that Dearmer approached her with his request, with which she willingly complied. She was by now spiritually settled and because she was also very musical the tune instantly appealed to her, she produced this joyful song celebrating not only the creation as told in Genesis, but the new creation of every fresh day: "God's re-creation Of the new day". This hymn conveys the freshness and joy to me that for many years Haydn had done in his immortal 'Creation'.

KATE BARCLAY WILKINSON

I am trying as far as possible to group together hymns and writers which have something in common. We come now to two devoted Christian ladies who have each produced a notable hymn - notable at least to me, for both hymns made an instant impact on me when first hearing them.

First, 'May the mind of Christ my Saviour' (739 H. & P.). Based on Paul's words: "Let this mind be in you, which was also in Christ Jesus", it is a lovely meditation blending the thought of Christ dwelling with us and, arising from that indwelling, service for others in their need. Unfortunately we know very little about the authoress, Kate Wilkinson (1859-1928), even the date of her birth being conjectural, but we do know that she was a member of the Church of England and a few pointers indicate that she was of the evangelical wing, probably a member of the Clapham Sect, like Katherine Hankey (q.v.). Like her she was deeply involved in evangelistic work among girls. As to her character, I can only point to the internal evidence of this hymn. I suggest you read it through and ask two questions: "Could anyone write words like this and not be a loving, out-and-out servant of her Saviour and of all she knew?"; and "Could I honestly say these words of myself?"

I fell for the second tune, 'St. Leonard's (Gould)' before I knew its history and when I found out something about it I knew why it was written for it. We know much about the composer, Rev. A. C. Barham Gould, except his youth. His birth was not registered in England, so it is assumed he was born abroad; it is also thought - there seems a lot of guesswork here - that he entered Ridley Hall Theological College about 1924, which would make him in his early thirties. By 1927 we are on surer ground, for by then he was curate of All Souls, Langham Place and his persuasions were very much the same as dear old Katie Wilkinson's. Forgive my speculating - did they know one another, did she look with approving eye on this promising young man who was going to enter college, or even before that and did she give him these verses to set to music? Perhaps some reader will enlighten me.

ROSAMOND E. HERKLOTS

The other hymn which impressed me at first sight was 'Forgive our sins as we forgive' (134 H. & P.) by Rosamond Herklots (1905-1987). It is one of the most recurring themes in the teaching of Jesus that it is hypocrisy to ask God to forgive us our sins if we harbour bitterness, certainly if we plan revenge, against anyone who has wronged us. The hymn starts with the phrase from the Lord's Prayer, "Forgive us our sins as we forgive those who sin against us" - direct enough, indeed, but reinforced by the story of the unforgiving servant and by the example of Jesus on the Cross. All this was brought home with renewed force on first meeting this hymn.

The writing of these verses is an interesting story. Rosamond was born in India but came to England for her education, going on to Leeds University to train as a teacher. She wrote a number of hymns but this is the one by which she is really known. She says that the idea came to her when she was over 60 years of age. She had a nephew of whom she was very fond and he had dug and planted his garden with beautiful flowers, but the rank weeds, docks, dandelions, etc., which had not been eradicated, were growing again, choking the loveliness of the borders. As she had time to spare and he was pressed with business and family matters, she set about the task of trying to clear the ground without disturbing the plants too much. One by one she loosened the tap roots and was getting them right out. As she was working the thought came to her that the bitterness and resentment in our minds were like these deep tap roots; in her own words, "How deeply rooted they were, hindering the growth of the flowers near them, just like the old resentments in our lives". What a jewel of thought when doing a boring and backbreaking job!

Rosamond submitted the verses to the parish magazine of her Church, St. Mary's, Bromley and they were soon taken up by several new hymn-books. I wonder how many bitter situations have been sweetened by these wonderful verses?

Chapter 15

INDEBTEDNESS TO THE WORLD CHURCH

One of the new facts of our time is the exchange of ideas between the Home Church and the Church Overseas. Initially it was a one way traffic - our brave missionaries taking the gospel to foreign lands, which is something we must never forget. There are places where the record of missions can only be described as heroic; young folk dying after only a few years work, but always someone else ready to take their place, hostile climate and sometimes hostile people, too, yet the assurance that they had a Saviour to offer these people sustained those men and their cause.

That was before my time, but I have had the privilege of knowing a few 'pioneer missionaries' who travelled inland to find a suitable base, where they erected a hut, and with their own hands built a church and compound with living quarters, in the process teaching native helpers skills of carpentry and bricklaying. All this sandwiched between learning the language, teaching the gospel, and healing the sick. "Where did you get your knowledge of medicine?" I asked one of these old-timers. "Oh, of course we had a three-month crash course on medicine and elementary surgery, then we learnt as we went along!" was the astounding reply. Well, those days are over and we honour the tenacity these men demonstrated.

There were mistakes made, one of which was to take our English hymns and teach them to these people, forgetting that our culture was not necessarily part of the Christian faith. That is an admission from one who is an enthusiast for the glorious legacy of English (and Continental) hymnody.

THOMAS STEVENSON COLVIN

I now want to think of three men who have learned this lesson, listening to local songs and adapting them to fit Biblical texts and most

109

important, encouraging native talent to produce their own lyrics and tunes. A flood of these have now come back to us, enabling us to worship in the idiom of other nations.

When 'Hymns and Psalms' was new to us we were visited by an enthusiastic little lady missionary who prevailed on us to sing 'Jesu, Jesu' (145 H. & P.), only she said to be authentic we should sing, 'Yesu, Yesu'. It is strange, as I look back, how difficult we found it to turn ourselves into Ghanaians at first, but how much we enjoyed it once we had the feel of singing this round a fire in the open air. This was the right way to think of it, for the author was conducting a course for evangelists at Chereponi (after which the tune is named) in Ghana, as part of their training. It is based on a local song, and one can easily imagine these new Christians taking up this tune they knew, one singing the verses and all responding with the name Yesu, their new Saviour and Lord.

What kind of a man was this who could produce this synthesis of the Christian message with the culture of Ghana? Born in 1925, he was baptised Thomas Stevenson Colvin, went to school in his native Glasgow and won a place at Glasgow Technical College to train for what he wanted to do, to be an engineer. From there he went on to Glasgow University and gained his B.Sc.

By then the War was under way and Tom was sent to Singapore and Burma to serve with the Royal Indian Engineers, rising to the rank of Lieutenant because of his previous qualifications. On returning to Scotland, he was feeling a call to fulltime service for Christ and in 1948 entered Trinity College to study for the ministry. He left three years later and was licensed as a probationer minister in the Church of Scotland. During this period he was associated with the Student Christian Movement and the Iona Community.

He was ordained in 1954 and immediately sent to Malawi as associate minister of Blantyre Presbyterian Church. There he was Headmaster of the mission school and secretary for education. Later he was appointed General Secretary of the Blantyre Synod but could not take up this post as the Welensky Government declared him a prohibited immigrant. Consequently he was moved to Ghana to do pastoral, evangelistic and social work (for which he was renowned). With a change of government he was recalled to Blantyre to lead a massive social programme sponsored by his Church and he laboured on there until 1976 when a suitable Malawian was found to succeed him. He decided to retire to England, happy in the knowledge that the work he loved would now be carried on by a man to whom the local people could relate better than any European.

He was appointed leader of a team ministry at Sydenham United Reformed Church and his unrivalled experience of famine relief, aid to refugees, health, education and youth work, made him much sought after by relief agencies all over the world, involving him in ceaseless travelling. With his experience of searching out Ghanaian music and songs he compiled several collections of them. Of this particular hymn Tom Colvin says: "Hearing this melody I thought it would be a suitable vehicle for a song about God's love for all of us, it had to be about black and white, rich and poor. I was ashamed of the wasteful affluence of my people, but proud of the Gospel that transforms us into servants of one another."

CARL DERMOTT MONAHAN

'Jesus the Lord said, I am the Bread' (137 H. & P.) is a similar hymn but in a different idiom, coming from India. Carl Monahan (1906-1957) was born in India, of Methodist Missionary parents, but came to England to receive his secondary education at Kingswood School, from which he passed to Trinity Hall, Cambridge, graduating M.A. He went on to Ghana (then the Gold Coast), serving in the Colonial Service, before returning to England to train for the ministry. He returned to India as education officer and rose to be Principal of Andhra Union Theological College and he wrote several books on the languages of India. He met another Missionary, Kate Greenfield, who was enthusiastically collecting words and music of native hymns in Indian dialects. She showed him this hymn among others and he translated it into English.

It is, he says, a good teaching hymn, used in Indian Christian schools, based as it is on the titles which our Lord gave himself in St. John's Gospel (chapter 6, etc.). The original was the work of an unknown Indian Christian. Mr. Monahan notes that it is a good example of the way Indian teachers get home Christian teaching to their pupils - and to those who are illiterate. The tune had to be produced in western notation.

Mr. Monahan was a fine linguist, who wrote many books in the native languages. Sad it is that such a gifted and scholarly man should only live to the age of 51, when he was opening up the Christian gospel to India so effectively.

The tune 'Yisu Ne Kaha' is the Urdu melody originally associated with the words, simply and effectively harmonised by Rev. Francis Westbrook.

TAI JUN PARK

We move on to a hymn from the other side of the world, Korea, a country which has known the horrors of war. The hymn is 'The Saviour's precious blood Has made all nations one' (410 H. & P.). I remember singing it for the first time; it was Armistice Sunday and I must admit I went unwillingly to Church. Was there going to be even a hint of glorification of war? Knowing our minister I could not imagine there would be, but I did not like these services either as a worshipper or as a preacher, for reasons that will be obvious from the first chapter of this book. Imagine, therefore, the means of grace this hymn was to me. As usual, I wondered, what made this man - with such a peculiar name, Tai Jun Park - write it? My inquiries led me into one of the most interesting stories, or series of stories, that I have come across.

Dr. Park (1900-) was a Professor teaching at the University of Seoul, S. Korea, when a Christian student came to him to ask for a Korean hymn to take to an international youth rally in India, these verses were the result. Two years later Dr. Park travelled to America and was surprised to see the hymn in English in a college magazine. It transpired that it had previously come into the hands of an ageing missionary, Dr. William Scott, who had made the English translation, not knowing its origin, with the help of a female teacher, Yung Oon Kim. Was she the one who found the Korean version? We don't know anything about her, or what part she played in all this, but we do know something about the two men. Dr. Park was Korean-born, and was educated at Union Christian College, but travelled to America to complete his education at the Westminster Choir College, Princetown, New Jersey. He returned to his native land to teach at Yonsei Christian University, Seoul, where he rose to be Dean of the College of Music. Did we know there were such Institutions in South Korea?

I well remember when the Korean war started, a friend being shown a paper with a picture of some of the fighting in Seoul and remarking, "I didn't know much about the place, but I pictured a lot of mud huts - but look at these magnificent buildings!" This was where Dr. Park spent his life teaching music as a vehicle of the Christian message with such distinction that he was awarded his Honorary Doctorate by Wooster College, Ohio. All this was carried on during war and the threat of war. It would be several years before any semblance of peace would be restored when he wrote these verses. Having an even greater horror of war than I had, with it all around him, this was a cry from the heart:

112

"In this sad world of war
Can peace be ever found?
Unless the love of Christ prevail,
True peace will not abound."

Dr. Scott, on the other hand, came from Scotland. He responded to a call by Dr. MacMillan for young men to go to Canada to train for the ministry and also as missionaries, as there was then a severe shortage of both for the opportunities open. He graduated at Kingston University and took theology at Westminster Hall, Vancouver. He then married and in 1914, with his wife, went to Korea where they settled down to a life of preaching, teaching and training colporteurs - lay Bible teachers who were destined to travel far and wide, even reaching well into China. He was Principal of a High School, but resigned as soon as he had trained a native Korean to take over. He then repeated these tactics, for he firmly believed (like Tom Colvin, q.v.) that the people to whom he had been sent would respond to one of their own countrymen better than to a foreigner. So admired was he for what he had done for education that he received many Government honours for his outstanding leadership.

Then came World War II, when he was interned in his own home. He was one of only four who were even allowed to stay, because of outstanding service to the nation, all others being repatriated as undesirable aliens. So in a small way he could continue his work by teaching and encouraging people who came to his home. Later he, too, was repatriated to Canada, to a hero's welcome, and being honoured by Union College, Vancouver, who conferred on him a Doctorate of Divinity. Here he served his only Canadian pastorate until 1946 when, at the cessation of hostilities, all missionaries were allowed to return. Imagine the devastation left behind by the war. Dr. Scott was now aged 60, when many men would gladly retire; but no - he threw himself into evangelistic work, visiting many refugee camps, and 'in his spare time' organising the distribution of food and other relief, and even supervising the building of a hospital.

In the midst of all this activity there was a regrettable episode. Dr. Scott's theology had always been moderately 'liberal', and a fundamentalist group within his own church charged him with heresy, totally ignoring his zeal, his love for his people and his many converts. In spite of this move against him, he soldiered on, with characteristic love and forbearance, until he retired at the age of 70.

113

He still continued to speak, preach and write on behalf of the missionary work he loved, raising funds for its continuance. Then at the great age of 90 he was requested by the Board of World Missions of the United Church of Canada to write a book telling of his life and work and the exploits of him and his colleagues in that distant land in the throes of conflict. He called it quite simply 'Canadians in Korea'.

Dr. Park's hymn, translated by Dr. Scott, is a plea for peace - a peace that will only come as we learn to do Christ's will, especially obeying his command "As I have loved you, so should you love one another." This hymn has opened my eyes to heroic work being done for the Master in a part of the world little known to me.

HARRY EMERSON FOSDICK

There has been a large and varied contribution to our hymnody from across the Atlantic - hymns which have come to stay. Let us first look at a hymn of a generation ago which, although written for a special occasion, is applicable to later crises or difficulties. It is 'God of grace and God of glory' (712 H. & P.), by Harry Emerson Fosdick (1878-1969).

This is a name taking me back to my boyhood with memories of eager, forward-looking young preachers quoting him in their sermons; "as Dr. Fosdick says" often cropped up. He was then the apostle of youth, the symbol of progress. In those days between the wars he seemed to be throwing off old ideas like fusty old Edwardian clothes. His books were sold in thousands: 'The Manhood of the Master', 'A Guide to Understanding the Bible' and 'The Meaning of Prayer' were some of them. The latter was suggested fairly recently as the basis of a study session at our Local Preachers' Fellowship. I think some of us thought it rather 'old hat' but when we studied it we found it thoroughly up-to-date. We found we could pick up second-hand copies almost anywhere. Perhaps I should have re-phrased the above remark: "sold by the million".

When Harry Fosdick had graduated and taken theological training he was ordained as a Baptist minister. Alongside his first pastorate he taught at two theological colleges and in 1918 he accepted the post of associate minister of a fine new Presbyterian Church. It was while he was here that he met opposition (like Dr. Scott, q.v.) from a fundamentalist group. It seemed they could not fault him on anything like the divinity of Christ, or even who wrote the Pentateuch, but on ecumenical matters! To a man so sought after this did not cause much anxiety, he just resigned and took pastoral charge of another new Church, this time Baptist once again. As well as attracting great congregations, he embarked on broadcast preaching, thus widening his influence still further. He also travelled to Britain and the Far East on preaching tours.

With all this success Fosdick still felt he was being restricted by the rather strict Baptist tradition of his Church and the fact that he was ministering mainly to the wealthy. His misgivings became known to possibly the richest man in America, John D. Rockefeller, who offered to build a magnificent new Church wherever he wanted it. Fosdick insisted it must be in the poorest district of New York, and so it was; the famous Riverside Church was his. It was opened in 1930 and this hymn was written for the dedication. He said of it: "It was more than a hymn to me; it was a very urgent personal prayer. For with all my hopeful enthusiasm about the new venture there was inevitably much humble and sometimes fearful apprehension." Why this trepidation, we might wonder? He had had success that many ministers might envy, but he was basically a very humble man. He spent the remainder of his working life there, doing what he had longed to do at his previous Churches, to minister to the poor and needy. We see his 'urgent personal prayer' in the words repeated in each verse:-

"Grant us wisdom,
Grant us courage,
For the facing of this hour."

This was a turning-point in Fosdick's life, but these words have been, and still will be, sung at critical turning-points in world and personal affairs.

KAREN LAFFERTY

Still in the United States, we turn from a distinguished scholar and leader of thought to writers of hymns still living and whose works have a new feel about them. Mainly the hymns consist of scriptural texts skilfully arranged together, set to good lively tunes. I feel that the work of these composers is reminiscent of teaching hymns like the Urdu hymn 'Jesus the Lord said . .' (137 H. & P.) quoted a few pages back. Is this not a feedback of earlier missionary enterprise?

Particularly attractive is 'Seek ye first the kingdom of God' (138 H. & P.). Here are two sayings of Jesus and a quotation of his from

Deuteronomy, strung together and set to tuneful music — all the more effective when the refrain is sung as a two-part round. In 'Hymns & Psalms' this is printed in the upper register of the bass clef and may be taken by alto ladies, or men's voices, or by instruments.

This hymn is by Karen Lafferty (b. New Mexico, date unknown). Of her early life we know nothing except that she was a University student who seems to have opted for the life of a roving musician. She eventually arrived in California, where she found the Maranatha Music movement in full swing. She entered into this with great enthusiasm, later moving on again to 'the old world' to found her own 'Musicians for Mission' movement based at Amsterdam.

DON FISHEL

Another good hymn of the same type is 'Alleluia, alleluia, give thanks to the risen Lord' (250 H. & P.). Its title indicates that it is based on the Resurrection of our Lord; but also on his death as being symbolic of the believer's death to sin and rising again to new life in Christ. Again it consists of a series of quotations from the Bible, set to a hearty tune by Don Fishel (b.U.S.A., 1950). He, too, was a University student seeking to express his Christian faith in sound theological quotations, with a catchy tune. He insists that as these texts occurred to him the music came to him at the same time. There is a spontaneity about the whole piece that makes this quite credible.

Many hymns of this type are of unknown origin and not always as good as those we have considered. Some are very trashy and one wonders why room is found in 'Hymns and Psalms' for them. They are often full of 'vain repetitions'. I cite 'He's got the whole world in his hand' (25 H. & P.) as an example of dragging one good thought into a whole hymn. (Please don't write if you disagree - we are all entitled to our opinions!). 'Give me joy in my heart' (492 H. & P.) is a better type, but are we to keep praising till the *break* of day!? It seems that the original words were 'Give me oil in my lamp, keep it burning till the break of day'. This makes sense, who altered it?

BETTY JANE PULKINGHAM

A name associated with modern hymns is Mrs. Betty Pulkingham (b.U.S.A., 1928), who has collected and arranged them from many sources. She has been co-editor of three modern books:- 'Sound of Living Waters', 'Fresh Sounds' and 'Cry Hosanna', and all her arrangements are included in these books. She was born and educated in North Carolina and taught music theory at the University of Texas. In 1951 she married Rev. W. G. Pulkingham, of Houston, Texas. They moved to Scotland in 1971 and here began the production of these new books. They also formed a group under the name of 'The Fisherfolk', to make recordings and conduct revival campaigns using these new hymns.

We have some of these in 'Hymns and Psalms', some of which are anonymous, like 'O what a gift! What a wonderful gift!' (270 H. & P.), with its easily learnt refrains and slightly irregular verses which trace the birth, death and resurrection of Jesus in a most dramatic way. This impressed me immediately and I found it best to give the verses to a good soloist who could give full expression to them, while all the others joined in the chorus. In this way the congregation could join in effectively on the next occasion.

Some of these songs have the disadvantage of being on several pages, making it necessary to turn back and forth a lot (pity the poor organist!). This difficulty is present in 'I am the Bread of Life' (611 H. & P.). It is a design fault which I feel could have been avoided - but I will pass on. 'I am the Bread of Life' is different from most hymns of this style, which so far have all been Protestant and Evangelical in origin. But here we have the first two Roman Catholic ones. It is notable that since Vatican II the Catholic Church has embraced the modern idiom to a surprising degree. This hymn consists of a series of texts from St. John's Gospel, with a definite Catholic tone. It was written and composed by Suzanne Toolan, a sister of Mercy from California and arranged by Betty Pulkingham.

SEBASTIAN TEMPLE

Probably the most popular modern Catholic hymn is "Make me a channel of your peace' (776 H. & P.). This 'prayer of peace' was attributed to St. Francis of Assisi, though doubt has been cast on this assumption, but evidently the author/composer of the hymn accepted the old authorship, for he was a member of the Franciscan Community in Los Angeles. His full name was Johann Sebastian Templehoff (b. S. Africa, 1928), which he shortened to Sebastian Temple. Born and educated in South Africa, he described himself as a High School drop-out. He seems to have travelled here and there - Britain, India and the United States (how did these roving characters support themselves, let alone pay for travel?). Suffice it to say he arrived in Hollywood - an unlikely place for conversion - and became a Catholic. He took his new-found faith very seriously, taking part in a mission to the down-and-outs in Mexico and then went to Los Angeles to work with the Franciscan Brothers in the down-town part of the city. It was here he composed and sang his songs for use in his mission work composing several albums.

He had long wanted to set the 'Prayer of St. Francis' to music, but could not get going with it. One day he was having another try and, feeling frustrated, he turned to a small model of St. Francis saying "I can't do this, if you want it, you do it." He made a cup of tea to console himself, picked up his guitar, set the tape recorder running, and it just poured out. He made a few impromptu alterations to the words to fit the tune, the main one being 'channel' instead of the usual translation 'instrument'. I mention this because 'channel' was a word Martin Luther often used to stress the point that we are only the means by which God's grace flows to other people, it is not our grace, but God's. So a Friar used a Lutheran word to express a thought that would conquer the world.

While still thinking of our indebtedness to the World Church, I feel I must make brief reference to two men of great influence who have given us hymns which have made a deep impression in this country.

Firstly there is Nayaran Tilak (1862-1919) who has given us a devotional gem:-

> One who is all unfit to count
> As scholar in Thy school.   (H. & P. 539)

We shall meet him a little later on - his story is fairly well known. He was on a train journey to a new job as a librarian when he got into conversation with an unknown missionary about books in general. When they parted the missionary gave him a New Testament advising him to read about Jesus the Saviour of the world - the reading of it led to him becoming a Christian and devoting the rest of his life to spreading the gospel.

In his words "I could not tear myself away from those burning words of love, tenderness and truth. Here in the Sermon on the Mount is the answer to the most abstruse and profound problems of Hindu philosophy." So a devout and learned Hindu became a dedicated Christian teacher.

The other great Christian who has given us some fine hymns came from Ceylon (as it was then) - Dr. Daniel Niles (1908-70). He was a real statesman of the World Church, his influence being felt in the World Conferences at Amsterdam, Geneva and Upsala, yet he remained a humble believer, writing popular books and devotional poems.

I shall refer to "Father God in heaven" (H. & P. 518) later but I would also like to recommend "Father in heaven" and "The great love of God" (H. & P. 3 & 45).

Chapter 16

MORE MODERN STYLE HYMNS

DAVID MANSELL

We now leave those popular modern hymns coming to us from over-seas and turn back to our own country, for there are people who have produced successful hymns here, too. I take as an example 'Jesus is Lord' (260 H. & P.). It is obviously of the same type, except that Scripture is not so much quoted as paraphrased. The first verse reminds us of Psalm 8: "When I consider thy heavens, the work of thy fingers, the moon and the stars, which thou hast ordained . . ."; while verses 2 and 3 recall Paul's wonderful words in Philippians, chapter 2 - generally accepted to be a credal hymn of the early Church which Paul quotes to drive home his point.

The whole hymn is by David Mansell (b. 1936), who graduated in physics and worked for some years, when the urge to work full time preaching the Gospel was so strong that he gave up his job for evange-listic work. So here we have a fine statement of our faith from both the Old and New Testaments.

MARY BYRNE / ELEANOR HULL

There are four hymns in 'Hymns & Psalms' which are linked by asso-ciation with the old traditional tune 'Slane', in fact all seem to have been written with this tune in mind. Curiously their metres are designated 11.11.11.11; 10.11.11.11; and irregular!

The original hymn to be set to this tune was 'Be thou my vision' (378 H. & P.). It was first in M.H.B. in a form that was difficult to sing, but has been replaced by a more straightforward version, for which we are indebted to the B.B.C. Hymn Book. The words are a translation of a very ancient Irish poem, possibly 8th century, by Mary Byrne (1880-1931), a great expert on ancient forms of Erse. She rendered it in prose and another lady, Eleanor Hull, (1860-1935) an expert on Irish literature, saw it and thought it could be versified to make a good hymn. And so it remained for some years.

JAN STRUTHER

Later, Percy Dearmer thought the tune 'Slane' might be used for new words and as we have seen in the case of Eleanor Farjeon he had a habit of approaching Christian novelists or poets to turn their talents to writing hymns for the projected 'Songs of Praise'. He thought of Jan Struther (1901-1953), the author of that celebrated book 'Mrs. Miniver' - later to be made into a film. (Incidentally, Jan's name was made out of her initial and her maiden name: J. Anstruther). She liked the tune too and produced 'Lord of all hopefulness' (552 H. & P.), which she called the 'All day hymn' from the last line of each verse: 'the break', 'the noon', 'the eve' and 'the end of the day'.

However, not everyone was so sure that it was a good idea to set more words to this old tune. Canon Cyril Taylor, who has given us many fine new metrical tunes, thought 'Slane' should be kept for 'Be thou my vision', so he wrote a new tune for Jan Struther's hymn and very appropriately called it 'Miniver' after her famous book. 'Hymns & Psalms' carries both tunes, so you can take your pick. 'Miniver' is certainly a fine tune, worth learning.

BRIAN WREN

The usefulness of the tune 'Miniver' is not confined to the one hymn mentioned above, for it is also set to Brian Wren's very original harvest hymn 'Praise God for the harvest of farm and of field' (351 H. & P.). I call it original, for what other hymn praises God for harvests from afar, for minerals beneath the ground, for the research of scientists and for many such unusual things, concluding with thanks for those who struggle to conquer oppression, so that God's harvest of justice and peace may be gathered?

Dr. George Caird told me to "watch out for Brian Wren - he is the man of the future". Born in 1936, he became one of Dr. Caird's boys at Mansfield College, after graduating at New College, Oxford. He seems to have held only one pastorate when his exceptional gifts were recognised and he became - among much else - an educational consultant, a worker for the Third World and War on Want. He has written many hymns already and published books on hymns, education, peace and other subjects. There are ten of his hymns in 'Hymns & Psalms', each one fresh, modern, yet good sound stuff.

JACK WINSLOW

Back to the tune 'Slane': far from being reserved for one hymn, it has been pressed into service for yet another hymn, 'Lord of creation, to you be all praise!' (699 H. & P.) by Jack Winslow (1882-1974). This is another good hymn of praise to God for all his attributes - power, wisdom and so on, with just that little bit of judicious repetition to give coherence to the whole hymn.

Jack Winslow was educated at Eton and Balliol College, Oxford, and was ordained after training at Wells Theological College. After serving for some years in this country he was sent to India on behalf of the S.P.G., where he worked as a missionary for 19 years. He became an authority on the Christian approach to Hinduism, gaining much of his insight into this problem from his knowledge of that extraordinary character, Narayan V. Tilak, (q.v.) who urged his fellow Hindus to follow Christ, the supreme Guru, and opened his house as the ashram. He intended to write a life of Christ in Marathi verse but died at the age of 57, having completed only a fraction of it.

Tilak had succeeded in partially breaking down the barriers between Christianity and Hinduism, a work that could be carried on by men like Winslow, who wrote several books, including a life of Tilak. After his return to England, Jack Winslow acted as Chaplain at Bryanston School, then at Lee Abbey, and retired at the astonishing age of 80, but then still able to enjoy 12 years full retirement!

Winslow's hymn has an alternative tune 'Tarporly' - a good tune which I have not heard sung. It is by Martin Ellis, who has given us several other new tunes. He is currently Director of Music at Reigate Grammar School and Organist at St. Martin's Anglican/Methodist Church, Dorking. He says he wrote this tune while invigilating an examination. What a good idea!

TIMOTHY DUDLEY-SMITH

In addition to the vast numbers of 'popular' rhythmic hymns now being produced, there are many people - mainly ministers and clergy of all denominations - writing new texts in metrical form. One outstanding man is Timothy Dudley-Smith (b. 1926), famous for one hymn above all the others he has written: 'Tell out, my soul, the greatness of the Lord' (86 H. & P.). It is thought that this is the most widely used of all modern hymns.

The author was impressed when he opened his 'New English Bible' and read the familiar 'Magnificat', the complete freshness of the translation, while being faithful to the original Greek, induced him to use it word for word as the first line of a new hymn. He went on to base the later verses on Mary's song, ending by repeating the first line and adding the last line of the N.E.B. translation. Carried along by Walter Greatorex's fine tune, no wonder it has become so popular.

Timothy was certainly a remarkable boy, expressing the desire to be a Christian minister at the age of 11. I doubt whether many of us have such clear-cut convictions as young as that. Speaking personally, as a child I disliked ministers, however nice they were to me. I don't think I had ever heard Rev. Sidney Smith's dictum that there were three sexes, men, women and clergymen - but I thought they were a race apart, a peculiar people! It pulled me up when *I* was a young preacher and trying to encourage some boys in that way and I suggested to the most hopeful lad that he might think of going 'on trial'. There was a pause and I half regretted the words I had spoken when he said quite deliberately, "Yes, I must do that, you see, I want to go on to be a minister". He stuck to it, and so did young Timothy, who passed his M.A. at Cambridge and went on to Ridley Hall for theology. After ordination he served in several parishes before being appointed Archdeacon of Norwich, then Suffragen Bishop of Thetford. He is strongly evangelical, even in his young days having headed the Cambridge University Mission in Bermondsey; and he served as Editorial Secretary of the Evangelical Alliance for several years. He heartily supported the Billy Graham Crusades and was founder / editor of the magazine 'Crusade'. In all Timothy Dudley-Smith has written about 100 hymns and a book entitled 'Someone who Beckons'.

Regrettably, with the exception of 'Tell out my soul', few of his hymns are regularly sung - at least in my experience. I wonder if this is because he sometimes uses unusual metres and the tunes set to them are not easy. 'Spirit of God within me' (294 H. & P.) is an example. It is a great hymn, using what I have called 'repetition with a difference' to give unity to it: "Spirit of God - of truth - of love - of life". 'Ruach' is a good tune, but it needs some rehearsal, preferably with a good choir, to get it going. It is possible to sing it to the tune 'Beneath the Cross of Jesus' - not ideal, but better than a disaster.

The same cannot be said for 'Child of the stable's secret birth' (124 H. & P.). There is no alternative tune to suit a small congregation and of the two set tunes possibly Christopher Dearnleys is the more straightforward, although I think Valerie Ruddle - who can usually be relied on to give us a good tune - has done next best here, though the awkward irregularities will always be difficult to overcome. I recently heard of a lady preacher to whom this hymn appealed strongly and as she had three preaching engagements over the Advent period, in different churches, she felt she would like to share this hymn with the people. On the first occasion it was hardly a great success and on the second it was a total disaster (I am afraid I do not know which tune was attempted). On the third occasion she decided to ask the congregation to read the words with her - she felt it was just the blessing for which she had prayed.

I am sure there are some good lessons here for preachers, whatever their status; one is that we so often forget the value of reading in chorus, when we can concentrate our minds without having to give our attention to an unfamiliar and possibly difficult tune. I would urge preachers to read Mr. Dudley-Smith's hymns and use them, for the others do not present the same difficulties as these two, and they all have that quality which makes a hymn enduring.

CARYL MICKLEM

Another of our promising living hymn writers is the U.R.C. minister, Rev. T. Caryl Micklem (b. 1925). I was attracted by playing over his delightful little hymn 'Give to me, Lord, a thankful heart' (548 H. & P.), of which he is both author and composer. Then recently it was chosen by a U.R.C. minister and I expected the usual 'new hymn' reaction, he said the people might not know it and gave it a little boost, and lo and behold the hymn seemed to sing itself and everyone loved it. I am now far from young, but I can imagine children taking to it.

Another of his hymns, aimed deliberately at children, is 'Father, we thank you' (561 H. & P.), to which he has also written the tune, with the intriguing title 'All kinds of Light'. This is very apt, for the hymn is about the many kinds of light that brighten our lives, culminating in the love of Jesus, giving us hope for tomorrow through joy and sorrow. The two hymns reflect all the freshness of youth without being trivial.

Mr. Micklem is represented in 'Hymns and Psalms' by two more hymns for which he did not write the music and which can be sung to a suitable metrical tune. Both were written for special occasions and so could be rather limited in their usefulness. 'Thanks be to God, whose Church on earth Has stood the tests of time and place' (570 H. & P.) was written for the reorganisation of the Council for World Mission, seeking partnership with indigenous Churches - a process which must surely increase. There will be occasions when a forward-looking hymn like this will be an inspiration to sing.

'Father, your Church with thankfulness' (650 H. & P.) was written for an ordination of students and would make a great impression on any young person taking such a step as this.

Thomas Caryl Micklem was the son of Rev. E. R. Micklem, who at that time was Chaplain of Mansfield College, Oxford - which has figured several times in these reminiscences - the College where his son later received his own training. After his ordination he held pastorates in Northamptonshire before moving to the London area, later becoming minister of St. Columba's U.R. Church, Oxford.

He soon displayed his gift for writing and composing, especially hymns, in fact he has an enormous interest in hymnology.

BRIAN FOLEY

So far in this section I have not noted the contribution made by living Roman Catholic authors, and the one I would choose as the most notable is Brian Foley (b. 1919). A Liverpudlian, he trained for the priesthood at Upholland and was ordained in 1945. He has spent all his service in his own county and still ministers in Chorley. His hymns have a simple directness which makes an instant appeal - to me at least.

The first hymn that struck me is 'Holy Spirit, come, confirm us' (288 H. & P.). Here, behind the simplicity, are profound statements on the doctrine of the Holy Spirit's work, teaching the truth, acting as our advocate, renewing us, possessing us, and concluding with a concise statement of the nature of the Holy Spirit as in the Nicene Creed. The first time I sang it I realised that as a good Catholic he was affirming the 'Western' version of the creed, for the Latin word 'filioque' ('and the Son') was the point of controversy which split the Western (Roman) Church from the Eastern (Orthodox) Church in 589 A.D., for the latter insisted that the Holy Spirit proceeds from the Father alone, while the Western Church insisted on inserting the controversial 'and the Son'. The Church of England accepted this dogma, and as a Methodist I accept it too (via the Wesleys!) - but more because I believe in a Holy Spirit flowing not only from the Godhead, but from our Lord Jesus Christ, for he was God in the flesh, understanding our weakness, sufferings, hopes, fears, joys and sorrows. So I make this my creed each time I sing: "Holy Spirit of the Father, Holy Spirit of the Son."

The tune 'Drake's Broughton' is a particularly happy choice for the hymn, as Elgar was a Roman Catholic, in fact, he had a bit of a persecution complex about it, always imagining that he was passed over socially because of his allegiance to his faith - quite wrongly, I believe. He probably wrote this delightful little tune for St. George's R.C. Church, Worcester, where his father was organist. He must have liked it, for he later quoted it in his 'Nursery Suite'.

Fr. Foley stated his aim when writing a hymn was "to be guided as far as possible by Scripture and Theology". The one we have been looking at is firmly based on theology, but his other three hymns in 'Hymns and Psalms' are paraphrases of Scripture. One of these came to my notice recently when we sang 'With wonder, Lord, we see your works' (353 H. & P.). Here he takes thoughts from Psalm 8 and makes a beautiful hymn on the wonder of God's work in Nature.

His other hymns are:- 'Lord, as I wake I turn to you' (634 H. & P.), a real 'good morning' hymn, based on Psalm 5; and 'There is no moment of my life' (428 H. & P.), an effective and singable rendering of Psalm 139, that great meditation on the all-pervading presence of God. He has also published a delightful book:- "Sacred Words".

GEORGE B. CAIRD

From hymns based on the Bible it is only a short step to those about the Bible. When 'Hymns and Psalms' was still quite new I noticed how many new hymns there were about the Scriptures, the 'old stagers' were there, but also a wealth of new ones.

I have previously made mention of Professor George Caird (1917-1984), and his best-known hymn 'Not far beyond the sea' (477 H. & P.) is a fine hymn based on memorable Bible texts. The derivation of the first verse is perhaps not quite so obvious, it is a quotation from Pastor John Robinson's exhortation to the Pilgrim Fathers as they were departing on the daunting expedition on the 'Mayflower' from Plymouth in 1620. To encourage the faint-hearted he cried out "The Lord has more truth and light yet to break forth out of His holy word". What an important truth when so many are denigrating the authority of the Bible.

CHRISTOPHER MARTIN IDLE

One of the first of the new hymns on the Bible to catch my attention was 'Powerful in making us wise to salvation' (479 H. & P.). Throughout the hymn are all sorts of suggestive figures - "tool for employment", "compass for travel", "map in the desert" and "lamp in the dark".

>"History, prophecy, song, and commandment,
>   Gospel and letter and dream from on high;
>   Written by men borne along by the Spirit -
>   These are the Scriptures; on them we rely."

What a rich bunch of pictures to ponder on, and still more in each verse.

The author, Christopher Idle (b. 1938), after Oxford graduation and study at Clifton Theological College, served in Barrow-in-Furness, then moved to the London area and since 1976 has been vicar of Limehouse until moving to Oakley, Suffolk. He has published a book of modern hymns and one about modern hymns. He is an enthusiast on the preaching of George Whitfield and the Wesley Brothers and has published a book on that subject also, for he discovered that they worked in and around his parish.

I admit I was attracted to this hymn by its intrinsic value, but also by the magnificent Bach harmonisation of the old German tune 'Liebster Immanuel'. Unfortunately some people are put off by this and admittedly it isn't very easy. I was horrified, having seen the number on the hymn board at a recent service, to hear the organist strike up some other tune - but then I don't have any say in these matters now!

WILLIAM WATKINS REID

Some of the new hymns on the Bible have come to us from across the Atlantic. From the U.S.A. we have 'Help us, O Lord, to learn The truths your word imparts' (474 H. & P.). It is good, occasionally, to choose a hymn of this sort before a Scripture reading or between the reading and the sermon. In the past I have used something like Wesley's 'Come, Holy Ghost, our hearts inspire' (469 H. & P.) in this way; here is another one just as apt.

It was written by William Watkins Reid (b. 1923), whose father was a hymn enthusiast. William was set to be like him, but he was 16 when the 1939 War broke out, so later on, when his country joined in the War, he joined up and served in the Medical Corps and he was taken prisoner. On returning home again, he entered college, trained for the ministry and was ordained in the Methodist Episcopal Church. Since then he has ministered in various churches in the States. He has always been concerned with Christian education, which is reflected in this little hymn.

THOMAS HERBERT O'DRISCOLL

We go over the border into Canada for our next hymn: 'God, who hast caused to be written thy word for our learning' (472 H. & P.). This is a hymn in a rather different style with an unusual metre and some very long lines. It was written by T. Herbert O'Driscoll, an Irishman (b. 1928 in Cork). After education at Trinity College, Dublin, he was ordained and held one living there, then emigrated to Canada. He held many appointments there, the most important being Dean of Christ Church Cathedral, Vancouver. He served as an Anglican member of the committee preparing 'The Hymn Book' (Canada, 1971).

There he met Frederick R. C. Clarke, who was chairman of the sub-committee for the music of the book and they co-operated on this hymn. Mr. Clarke, three years younger than O'Driscoll, was the son of parents who had emigrated to Canada from England. He was a precocious student, qualifying as a Fellow of the Canadian College of Organists at the age of 21, and three years later obtaining his Mus. D. at Toronto University - the youngest ever to do so. He has since led a busy life as organist in various Churches also as conductor, lecturer and composer.

The tune he has produced for this hymn is not too difficult to pick up, in spite of its unexpected modulation halfway through, and the quick return to the home key for the last line.

REGINALD THOMAS BROOKS

There are still many hymns in this group of new items about the Bible which might be considered, and they are all welcome, for I think they indicate a renewal of interest in the Bible and acknowledgement of its authority as the basis of our beliefs and practices, but I will content myself with just one more: 'Thanks to God whose Word was spoken' (483 H. & P.).

I suggest you look at this very thoughtful hymn and see how much it claims for the Bible without claiming for it what it does not claim for itself. The author, Rev. R. T. Brooks (1918-1985), has used the device which I have previously referred to as 'repetition with variation'. Each verse begins with the words "Thanks to God whose Word . . .", after which the subject of the verse is introduced and enlarged upon. Then each verse ends with "God has spoken: Praise him for his open Word". So the Creation; the calling of the Jewish race; the Word in flesh, Jesus Christ; the Word revealed in the Scriptures through the ages; the Word translated into all languages and the Word still being revealed by the Holy Spirit, are all dealt with. I find the logical progression of thought in this hymn very satisfying, with its repeated 'refrains' to emphasise the oneness of its theme.

Of the two tunes set to it, I am not so sure. They are both good music, but neither was written for these words. I feel here a familiar tune would leave one's thoughts free to concentrate on the words of a hymn like this. I wonder if some organists will ignore the set tunes and do this? If they do, they should be careful not to use a tune inseparably joined to well-known words.

Reginald Brooks was brought up in the Congregational (now the United Reformed) Church. He entered the banking profession, but the call came to him to enter the ministry, and he trained at Mansfield College, Oxford. After ordination he served in Skipton and an inner city Church in Bradford, going on from there into what was to be his life's work - broadcasting - at the age of 31. His books 'Person to Person' and 'Communicating Conviction' reveal in their titles his concern for making the message of the Gospel intelligible to unbelievers.

The friends of Mr. Brooks speak of his reserved disposition and his gentle approach which covered an incisive mind. This, coupled with his ideal radio voice by which we shall remember him, all made him a really good broadcaster. He later went into T.V., but personally it is in radio that I remember him - I say remember because sadly he is no longer with us, having died while still in his 60s.

I wonder what it is that makes someone a good broadcaster? (I speak of radio, where the voice alone matters). Some wit has said "We prefer radio, the scenery is so much better" and there is a lot in this, for sound alone gives the imagination so much play. So often, with a good broadcaster, it can be a surprise - sometimes even a disappointment - to *see* them. I think of such diverse characters as Lionel Blue, Richard Harries and Donald English. I must stop waffling, for all this leads my thoughts on to how much broadcasting has enriched my love of hymns, via 'the Church at home'.

GEORGE HUGH BOURNE

One hymn which impressed me strongly, especially as I heard it twice in quick succession, was 'Lord, enthroned in heavenly splendour' (616 H. & P.). I looked it up in the index of 'Hymns and Psalms' and there it was, with the grand tune that I had heard, George C. Martin's 'St. Helen'. I must pause here to note that it was the tune which led me to this hymn, for in choral singing it is almost impossible to enunciate the words well enough for anyone listening to gather their meaning. I think there must be a lesson here; I listen to pop tunes crooned out in such a way that I can hear every word. Are there not soloists who could do the same for hymns, whose content is of so much more value?

However that may be, on reading the words of this hymn I found them to have that same grandeur as was conveyed by the music. Texts from Isaiah, the Gospels, Paul's sublime eloquence, and resounding notes of praise from Revelation, all combine to make a noble hymn of praise to our Saviour and Lord, Jesus Christ.

The author, George Bourne (1840-1925), after ordination, spent most of his career as a headmaster, until in later life he became Sub-Dean of Salisbury Cathedral. His hymns were written in his schoolmastering days and published as a book for use at St. Edmund's College, Salisbury. This is his only contribution to 'Hymns and Psalms', and his only hymn in M.H.B. was another less impressive one from the same book. This is not a new hymn, having been published in 1874, but broadcasting seems to have given it a well-deserved new lease of life.

Chapter 17

COMPOSERS AND TRANSLATORS

GEORGE THALBEN-BALL

Thinking of tunes coming over better than words, I found it a joy to hear a very old hymn sung to a tune by an old musical hero of mine, George Thalben-Ball (1896-1987), that redoubtable organist who was still playing with all his old gusto when he was nearly 90 - if my memory serves me right. His was an astonishing life, his first organ appointment being at the age of 15, and after several moves he went to the famous Temple Church in London where the standard of music was among the best in the country. The Church was destroyed by bombing in 1941, but it was eventually rebuilt and he supervised the construction of the new organ, resuming his duties ten years later. He was 81 when he retired! My memory of his playing is a stunning rendering of Handel's overture 'Athalia' on the organ of Birmingham Town Hall, where he was at that time City Organist. He was knighted for his outstanding services to music in 1982.

The tune I refer to is 'Arden', which he contributed to the B.B.C. Hymn Book and which I was glad to find in 'Hymns and Psalms'. It is set to the good old hymn of Isaac Watts, 'I'm not ashamed to own my Lord' (677 H. & P.). I was delighted, and it is an excellent vehicle for this fine hymn of commitment.

This is only one of several good tunes in the book contributed by Sir George Thalben-Ball, the others being 'Jesmian' (123), 'Kilgetty' (153), 'Arthog' (484), and several settings for canticles and psalms.

HENRY WALFORD DAVIES

Thinking of Thalben-Ball, my mind goes back to his distinguished predecessor at the Temple Church, the great Sir Walford Davies (1869-

131

1941), who left him such a dauntingly high standard in choral tradition to follow. He did not shine as an organ virtuoso so much as a choirmaster and composer of choral music. What many of my generation will remember most of all will be his amazing gift as a broadcaster. His talks on music, given with that comfortable voice of his and his unhurried, fatherly manner, could make music understandable to the least musical, without talking down to them, and still be interesting to the expert.

His other accomplishments were not so obvious to the general public, he had several posts as organist, leading up to his appointment as organist at the Temple Church, where he remained until 1923, when Thalben-Ball took over. He was appointed organist and master of the choristers at St. George's Chapel, Windsor, in 1927, but he was notable as well for his many-sided musical activities; teaching, adjudicating, conducting, and so on, including a Professorship of Music at Aberystwyth University (1919-26). How did he fit it all in? He was knighted while at the Temple Church, and in 1934 was honoured by being appointed Master of the King's Music, a position which he held until his death. In what little spare time he had he did a fair amount of composing, including organ music (his 'Solemn Melody' is still a great favourite), but mainly anthems, hymn tunes and Psalm settings.

We already knew (from M.H.B.) his fine setting of Addison's noble hymn 'The spacious firmament on high' (339 H. & P.), and his stately tune 'Vision', now set to Fred Pratt Green's 'It is God who holds the nations in the hollow of his hand' (404 H. & P.). This was originally written as an alternative tune to 'Mine eyes have seen the glory of the coming of the Lord' (242 H. & P.). There is also his inimitable setting of 'God be in my head' (694 H. & P.).

I have already dealt with some of the treasures that have come to my notice through the medium of broadcasting and two of Walford Davies's tunes I have heard on the Daily Service are among these. The setting to Psalm 121 (877 H. & P.), with its alternate solo and four-part lines, is enchanting - if you have never heard it you have missed something heavenly. Another hymn that struck me with its beauty was 'O King enthroned on high' (311 H. & P.). Again I could not hear all the words, so I was pleased when 'Hymns and Psalms' appeared, for me to play and sample the words and music for myself. My first impression was that, for something so lovely, it was all over too quickly; then I discovered that it originally had four verses, yet almost all hymnals omit the second verse:

"Yea, Thou art everywhere,
All places far and near;
O listen to our humble prayer,
Be with us here."

Why, I wonder? It seems to me to make for a continuity of thought between the present verses 1 and 2. What do you think? The hymn, as set to this Walford Davies tune, first appeared in 1904, but the original words of the hymn are very ancient, taken from a Greek service book of the 8th century, so we can move on from hymns made known through broadcasting to those which have come to us from very early times. This hymn, which belongs to both categories, is a good connecting link.

We have seen that there have been a number of scholarly men whose particular gift was to bring us devotional treasure from the past by their translations. The translator of 'O King, enthroned on high' is a lesser known man of this class, John Brownlie (1857-1925). He was a Glasgow man, educated at the University there, then gaining his D.D. at the Scottish Free Church College. After ordination he was appointed assistant minister at Portpatrick, Wigtownshire, taking full charge there at the age of 31. He quickly became interested in the affairs of the County, especially the education of the young, becoming a Governor of Stranraer High School and later their Chairman.

Brownlie's other great interest outside his pastoral work was the study of Latin and Greek hymnody of the early Church. He knew the work of Dr. J. M. Neale and others in this field and declared himself to be an unworthy successor to these men. In fact, he was acknowledged to be an authority on the subject and his profound learning was shown by his many books of translations from both languages and his researches into the origins of these hymns. In his own words, his ambition was "a very earnest desire to acquaint English readers with the valuable praise literature which lies buried in the service books of the Latin and Greek Churches" - an interest unusual for a minister of his Church.

GERARD MOULTRIE

I cannot really remember when I first heard the tune 'Picardy' - perhaps that was on the radio too - but again I was entranced instantly by its solemn beauty. I eventually found it in the English Hymnal - a book which I don't often use - but what a joy to play it again and again without particularly noticing the words set to it. Then 'Hymns and

Psalms' came along and I did take notice of the words: 'Let all mortal flesh keep silence' (266 H. & P.). The tune has an ancient sound, but is probably not earlier than the 17th century, set to a French carol, but the words, translated by Gerard Moultrie (1829-1885) are much earlier, from the Liturgy of St. James. This is thought to date from the 4th century and is still in use in the Orthodox Church.

Perhaps it is not strange that the tune 'Picardy', with its old-time atmosphere, is set in some hymn books to two other ancient hymns: 'Sing, my tongue, the glorious battle' (177 H. & P.), by Venantius Fortunatus (c. 535-600), the eminent Bishop of Poitiers who, though an Italian, born near Venice, ministered in France and wrote many hymns as well as secular poetry. The translator was our old friend, Percy Dearmer.

And the other hymn often sung to 'Picardy' is 'Sing, my tongue, the Saviour's glory' (624 H. & P.), written by the famous 13th century theologian, Thomas Aquinas (c. 1225-1274), in imitation of the older hymn. Both deal with the victory of Christ through his sufferings. It is noticeable that these early hymns, although spaced out by nearly a millenium, are in general objective, i.e. they concentrate on the attributes of the Godhead, without being overmuch concerned with human feelings, doubts, problems or faith. A good antidote for the over-sentimental type of hymn.

To return to No. 266, the translator, Gerard Moultrie, was a clergyman who devoted his life to teaching in boarding schools and colleges. He, too, was a lesser-known translator, but he compiled and published one book, 'Hymns and Songs for the Seasons and Saints' Days of the Church'. This included 'Let all mortal flesh keep silence', and many others from the Greek. There has been some controversy about the second verse of the hymn, with its reference to Mary. Why? There is no suggestion of worshipping her and the phrase 'in the body and the blood" in no way implies the doctrine of transubstantiation. It is, after all, a clear reference to chapter 6 of St. John's Gospel and it all depends whether you wish to interpret *that* literally or spiritually. However that may be, Percy Dearmer - surprisingly - has made a more Protestant version which is in some hymn books, but 'Hymns and Psalms' has stuck to the original.

However one views the second verse, the whole hymn is most impressive and moving. Its opening line sets the tone: "Let all mortal flesh keep silence, and with fear and trembling stand" - introducing a meditation on the mystery of the incarnation of our Lord.

ALFRED EDWARD ALSTON

I have always found a strong appeal in 4-line hymns which have the final line shorter than the rest. This line usually seems to produce a crisp statement summing up what has gone before. I have not spent much time or space in regrets about what we lost when 'Hymns & Psalms' was published, but I do sometimes wonder what the compilers were at when I realise some of the treasures of which we are now deprived. Take for example Pusey's free translation of verses from Lowenstern's poem: 'Lord of our life, and God of our salvation' (729 M.H.B.), a noble hymn enhanced by Barnby's equally fine tune 'Cloisters'. Here three 11-syllable lines are followed by one of only 5. One has only to sing this hymn to appreciate the effect I mean. Similarly Rawson's hymn to the Holy Spirit: 'Come to our poor nature's night' (297 M.H.B.), which has three 7-syllable lines followed by a 5. When sung to Jackson's 'Angelus' this effect was heightened by the fact that the last line was the same in each verse. These remarks apply equally to many hymns which happily are still with us, like Henriette Auber's 'Our blest Redeemer' (312 H. & P.) and Charlotte Elliott's 'Just as I am' (697 H. & P.). With these the phrase repeated at the end of each verse cannot fail to make its impact, whatever tune is used.

I have said all this because it is a joy to find two of the fine old 'French Church Melodies' in 'Hymns and Psalms': 'Ad Tuum Nomen' (5 H. & P.), set to words translated by Alfred Edward Alston; and 'Christe Sanctorum', which is set to no fewer than three hymns (H. & P. 455, 633 & 654). These two tunes, along with several others in the same metre, were introduced to Britain by Ralph Vaughan Williams in the 'English Hymnal' (1906). There they are set to ancient Office hymns dating from the 12th century, but in 'Hymns and Psalms' they are used for a variety of hymns, two ancient and two modern. These tunes were written in the ancient 'Sapphic Metre', with the emphasis on the first and penultimate syllables of each half-line, and the last line shortened to five syllables.

'Father, most holy, merciful and loving' (5 H. & P.) is a translation of a French hymn to the Holy Trinity, possibly dating back to the 9th century. The translator, Rev. A. E. Alston (1862-1927), was a Norfolk rector, who does not seem to have translated anything else. It was for inclusion in 'Hymns Ancient and Modern' (1904), but the version in 'Hymns and Psalms' has been considerably altered from the original. The hymn makes a fine, reverent opening for any service, not only on Trinity Sunday, with the tune 'Ad Tuum Nomen' making a stately accompaniment.

135

PERCY DEARMER

The tune 'Christe Sanctorum', as mentioned above, does duty for three hymns, two of which are modern, indeed by living authors who have been referred to elsewhere and who have had a prominent part in the recent surge of hymn writing. 'Christ is the world's Light' (455 H. & P.) is one of Fred Pratt Green's best, and 'Lord of the living' (654 H. & P.) is an impressive funeral hymn by Fred Kaan.

The third hymn to which this fine old tune is set is quite different. It is a morning hymn, of great age, translated by Percy Dearmer (who has translated no fewer than five hymns in H. & P.): 'Father, we praise thee, now the night is over' (633 H. & P.). This is thought to be by Pope Gregory, known as 'the Great' (545-604). There is some doubt about this, but it certainly dates back to around his time.

Pope Gregory was the one alleged to have seen a pathetic and bewildered group of children, torn away from their parents, and being offered in the market place in Rome as slaves. Impressed by their beautiful complexions and fair hair, he inquired about their nationality and was told they were Angles. "Non Angli, sed Angeli" ("Not Angles but Angels"), he is alleged to have replied. As a result he led a mission to 'Angleland' to bring Christ to these fair people. He was recalled, against his will, to be Pope, and his place to bring the message of the Cross to our shores, establishing the See of Canterbury, was taken by St. Augustine.

DUNCAN MACGREGOR

I had always looked on the Pope Gregory event as a red-letter day for England and I knew that, in the course of time, as missions reached further north and west, they met St. Columba's missionaries somewhere in the north of England. But it was a bit of a shock to find that a Scot - perhaps representing his race - declared that the Roman mission was a disaster, that Columba's men were well into Northumbria by the time Augustine arrived down south and that if they had been left alone they would soon have evangelised the rest of England in the name of the Celtic Church which was more democratic and certainly less authoritarian than Rome. There would have been no Council of Whitby and things would have been better all round. Well! Well!

All this leads me to point out that we also have a hymn attributed to Columba - at least it was one hymn which we now have divided into two - the translation of which we owe to Duncan MacGregor (1854-1923), who was a minister in Scotland and an authority on the early Scottish church. The two hymns are 'O God, thou art the Father' (52 H. & P.) and 'Christ is the world's Redeemer' (219 H. & P.).

Columba was indeed a contemporary of Augustine, starting as an Irish monk, converted - or some say partly converted - to Christianity by the Celtic Church, for he seems to have clung to some of the pagan religious practices and not been able to control his temper at first - as a Christian should. Still, by some means he became wholeheartedly for Christ, travelled to Iona and there founded a community of men who travelled far and wide spreading the Gospel. If only they had been left to carry on - according to my Scots friend.

JOHN CALVIN - ELIZABETH LEE SMITH

The linking of these ancient texts with great people who lived too long ago to dispute it, is a large subject. If they were not by the people stated, why have their names been connected with the words? Mainly I think because the doctrines or the sentiments expressed may seem to fit in with the characters of the supposed authors and it is possible that, if not written by the persons concerned, they were by a disciple or another member of the community they founded.

This leads me to a hymn 'I greet thee, who my sure Redeemer art' (391 H. & P.) which is alleged to be the work of John Calvin (1509-1564), and has been translated by Elizabeth Lee Smith. If it is Calvin's work, the character of this great man has been sadly misrepresented, but we do know that he was the author of 'The Institutes of the Christian Religion'. Born in Picardy, France, he studied for the priesthood, but while still young turned completely and fanatically against the Roman Catholic Church and became an extreme Protestant - much more so than Martin Luther, whose views were much more moderate. Could a man like this, who expressed his doctrines in all their severity in 'The Institutes', have written such tender verses? Fortunately recent research has thrown grave doubts on this and suggests that, although the hymn is in the 1545 Strasbourg Psalter which was edited by Calvin, these verses were probably by a disciple of his, or a minister in Strasbourg, who did not have his master's uncompromising views. There is no suggestion of original sin, even when speaking of the Kingship of Jesus. He is the King of mercy and of grace. The whole hymn is loving and lovable.

The English version is by Mrs. Elizabeth Lee Smith, whose work we have already seen in Lavater's 'O Jesus Christ, grow thou in me'. The tune set to it is 'Farley Castle', by Henry Lawes (1596-1662), which although written slightly later retains the Psalm-like flavour of the tunes used in Calvin's Psalter.

FRANCIS BLAND TUCKER

The thought of the French Psalter leads me on to a remarkable hymn, the tune of which is taken from one of them: 'Father, we give you thanks' (603 H. & P.). The tune 'Les Commandemens' was originally set to a French version of the Ten Commandments, hence its name. It is almost certainly by Louis Bourgeois, who did much of the musical work for Calvin in his Psalters. He was a composer in the sense that he more often took phrases of existing melodies and 'composed' them to form a continuous tune, than producing an original work. This method accounts for the fact that some of these old melodies often have a line which is reminiscent of something else. I find that congregations sometimes make hard work of the 6/4 bar in the first line, but compared with the rhythms of some modern tunes, this should present little difficulty.

It is, however, the words of this hymn which are impressive, for they are a translation of parts of one of the earliest documents of the Christian Church, some of which dates from the first century, but was completed in the second. There is evidence that it was read in the worship of the early Church, along with the Old and New Testaments - in fact before the canon of the new Testament was finally fixed. It contains a good deal of instruction for running the Church and ordering worship, which is pretty dry and out of date, but there are also prayers and devotional passages that are timeless.

It is called 'Didache Ton Dodeka Apostolon' ('The Teaching of the Twelve Apostles'), generally known by the first word only. It gives valuable insights into modes of worship and problems in connection with the ordering of the Church at a time when Peter and Paul were still remembered among the older members of the Churches. It was discarded as hardly worth a place in the New Testament, yet it is interesting for the view it gives into the life of the early Church.

Our English version we owe to an American scholar, Francis Bland Tucker (1895-1984), an Episcopal clergyman who has also given us some original hymns of real value. (See H. & P. Nos. 129, 253 & 371). I suggest you read particularly No. 371, a prayer for parents, who I am afraid we sometimes overlook in our prayers. It is, however, No. 603 that most impresses me, for it gives me the sense of the continuity of Christian worship.

All sorts of things have changed, some beyond recognition; yet human nature has not, nor has the instinct to worship - to worship God the Father, who planted the need for him in our hearts; Jesus Christ the Son, who is the spiritual counterpart of the daily bread, also God's gift; and the Holy Spirit, working through the Church, his body, uniting all believers; which will one day, like grain scattered, spread the final harvest over all the world.

Chapter 18

FINAL RANDOM THOUGHTS

There are those, of course, who say that Christianity is on its way out, complete with all its clutter, the Bible and the Church with its liturgies and hymnals, all soon to become museum pieces - relics of an over-credulous age. Science, they tell us, now accounts for that which was thought mysterious and supernatural - and so on. Really! All this has been said many times before and again and again a revival of faith has ensued. Happily not all scientists adopt this arrogant attitude, following rather the example of a scientist of a former age, Sir Isaac Newton, who declared: "I seem like a boy playing on the sea-shore . . . finding a smoother pebble or a prettier shell than ordinary, whilst the great ocean of truth lies undiscovered before me." Perhaps we *are* experiencing a period of 'religious recession', but it will pass if we - the Church - are faithful.

It has been said that there is no better cure for pessimism than the study of history, for in many parts of the world the Church, built up patiently over many years, has been swept away by enemies, only to stage a revival in greater strength later. The recurring message of Scripture is that setbacks may come, some so severe that all seems lost, but God is from everlasting to everlasting and will be victorious in the end.

Having said this, hymnals are not eternal, in fact very transitory. The previous Methodist one lasted 50 years (a record?), but 'Hymns and Psalms' does not seem set to be so long-lasting, in fact, although not much more than ten years old, it is already being supplemented by a flood of new small books representing the surge of new material, words and music; in the eyes of some rendering standard books obsolete. How are we to regard this massive inflow? I think it is a fair comparison to remember (if we are old enough!) how the 'Sankey' hymns in their day threatened to swamp the denominational hymnals, yet today they are just one contribution to the marvellous kaleidoscope of hymnody.

The new hymns of today are also largely imports from America and like the popular hymns of over a century ago are often of poor quality and very repetitious. It will be for coming generations to decide what is worthy to survive and be added to the glorious stock of sacred song. The same may also be said of the more traditional type of modern hymns.

HYMNS WE MISS

I wonder if I have given the impression that because I have found such joy over the years in discovering the riches contained in 'Hymns and Psalms' that I think it is the perfect hymnal. I do not think this is possible if one has definite opinions and tastes on any subject. I have often had to admit, when taking choir practice, "It's not my turn to be pleased!" So, if you don't wish to hear any criticism, don't read on! I have already expressed a few regrets for hymns omitted (e.g. see under A. E. Alston in previous chapter), so please be patient while I state a few more. I am thinking mainly as a preacher looking for hymns to drive home a point. This is why I advocated before its publication that 'Hymns & Psalms' should contain more hymns than was originally planned and I am glad that this was partially done. Even so, I have often found myself instinctively turning to look for words that had sprung to mind - a hymn that said just what I wanted - and disappointedly sighing: "Oh dear, it isn't there". As an instance, I was to preach on the general subject of Christian social service in the community, and I thought at once of Bishop How's 'We give Thee but Thine own' (923 M.H.B.). Turning it up to see exactly what it said, I found - "It's been omitted!" The odd thing is that modern authors have tended to make a fuss about the dearth of hymns on this theme - and undoubtedly they have produced some fine new hymns on the subject - but do any of them do better than this?

"To comfort and to bless,
To find a balm for woe,
To tend the lone and fatherless
Is angels' work below.

The captive to release,
To God the lost to bring,
To teach the way of life and peace,
It is a Christ-like thing."

Yet this has been jettisoned!

I am glad that we still have another of my favourites, F. M. North's "Where cross the crowded ways of life" (431 H. & P.), Charles Kingsley's "From thee all skill and science flow" (389 H. & P.) and Dean Plumptre's "Thine arm, O Lord, in days of old" (397 H. & P.). Predictably, we still have one of the lesser-known hymns of this type, Charles Wesley's "Jesus, the gift divine I know" (318 H. & P.).

Yet dear old Charles does not have it all his own way, I find. Twice I have heard on radio recently his hymn "O Love Divine, how sweet thou art" (434 M.H.B.). When it was announced my first thought was "What tune will they sing?" It always was difficult to know what suited these words best. They began to sing S. S. Wesley's 'Cornwall' (477(ii) H. & P.) - "A good choice", I thought; "I wonder what tune we have in the new book?" I took the book down from the shelf: "No, surely not! It isn't there!" Yet they are still singing it in the Church of England!

Thinking of Charles Wesley, how often in his hymns he uses not only Scriptural quotations, but a commentary on the quotation. The Lord's Prayer is an instance. Oddly enough, these familiar words are (so I am told) difficult in the Greek in many places. "Hallowed be thy name" is straightforward enough, although 'hallowed' is not a word in common use now; we know it means 'reverenced' or 'honoured'; but it is given deeper significance for me by a couplet in his hymn "God of all power" (726 H. & P.):

"Hallow thy great and glorious name,

And perfect holiness in *me*."

In the same way, "Lead us not into temptation" has always been a bone of contention and is now rendered "Do not put us to the hard test". Yet over two centuries ago Wesley wrote:

"But let us not be tempted

Above what we can bear."

This seems inspired insight to me, and the rest of the hymn (476 M.H.B.) is a fine exposition of these words - again omitted - will it return?

I recently went to a service where Addie was due to play and the preacher was discussing the hymns with her when they both said what a pity the "old" tune we loved was no longer in the book. The steward then said "We still have the old books here, why not sing it?, so we could have the tune we all love to the hymn 'O Master, let me walk with Thee'" (802 H. & P.). I know it wasn't set to those words, but at least it was in the

142

book. And so it was we dipped into the past singing WASHINGTON GLADDEN's (1836-1918) lovely hymn (again we are indebted to an American author) to a tune which, although written for another hymn, suits the words much better than the rather wooden 'Kettering' set to it. 'Stanley' (168 M.H.B.), as its name suggests, was written for Dean Stanley's great hymn on the Transfiguration 'Lord! it is good for us to be' - a hymn not much used, so we could hardly hope to have it retained. The tune, though, is another matter. Its composer, Dr. A. H. MANN, was a marvellous tunesmith, we still have 'Lasus' (562 H. & P.), 'Worship' (128ii H. & P.) and - new to 'Hymns and Psalms' - his alternative harmonisation of Gauntlett's 'Irby' (114 H. & P.). If you cast your mind back to the introit 'Once in Royal David's City' as it is sung at King's College Chapel, Cambridge, each Christmas Eve, with a single chorister singing the first verse - then for me comes the magical moment when the choir enter with these quite inspired chords, for verse 2. What may not be so well known is that Dr. Mann held the distinguished position of Organist and Master of the Choristers at that Chapel for the amazing period of 54 years, during which time he raised the standard of singing to the height it now enjoys.

ORGANISTS

So the Diary draws to its close. We are both in our eighties and not quite as active as we once were, with a few aches and pains to cope with, yet we have each other and we thank the loving God whose guidance we can trace for each new day of opportunity. Now living in a retirement home in a different part of the country - a little further west - we are still finding much fulfilling activity within our powers. It is for me a joy to preach the same Gospel as ever, once or twice a month and I hope, so long as my powers last, to continue adding the testimony of age to the message of our younger brethren.

I am fortunate that I have an understanding and constructive critic in Addie and if no-one else does, she will tell me when the time has come to retire. She, too, is kept busy playing organs and pianos here and there, with kind folk being willing to provide transport, as they do for me. But, I ask, "Should she have to?" Whereas young (and not so young) people are offering themselves to train as preachers, where are the new volunteer organists? Can I appeal to anyone who has the talent to offer himself or herself to fill these vacant places? There are several small Churches in *this*

Circuit - and I am sure the same applies elsewhere - who have no organist at all and would welcome an organist (or pianist - for there is a difference). Stand-ins for holidays, illness, etc. are difficult to find, also. I feel sure there may well be some who read this who have the talent to help out in this way. Services are held in country places which can hardly be to the glory of God - because singing has to be unaccompanied, often without any strong leading voices - which with sympathetic leadership could be a joy to the little congregation. Could I put out a plea for you to think of this?

Also as a preacher I have often been subjected to near torture by bad playing and I have gone back ten - even twenty - years later, to find the organist still making the same mistakes. On discreet enquiry I gather that the organ - or their own instrument - is never touched except on a Sunday! If any recognise themselves, may I say as gently as possible: "Is this the best you can offer to Almighty God?" With a bit of careful practice you never know what added blessing you can be.

PERSONAL USE OF HYMNS

So I could go on - for a Diary records impressions week by week - but I will conclude my random thoughts with a few observations about the personal use of hymns.

Have you tried committing a hymn that has impressed you to memory? If not, you may not realise what a blessing the words of a hymn can be in a time of quiet meditation and especially when sleep eludes you - as it must do with all of us sometimes. Whatever the reason for periods of insomnia - pain, illness, anxiety, or occasionally no apparent reason - I can recommend the old gag "If you can't sleep, don't try counting sheep, have a word with the Shepherd." Words of Scripture may come to mind, if not, why not try a hymn or two. In the past a number of hymns have been written for use at such times, but we should hardly expect to find these in a book intended for public worship, yet we still have good old Bishop Ken's 'Glory to thee, my God, this night' (642 H. & P.). He had troubles enough to make him include the lines:

"When in the night I sleepless lie,
My mind with heavenly thoughts supply."

Many have found Horatius Bonar's hymn 'O Love of God, how strong and true' (42 H. & P.) helpful in trying times. While it is mainly

144

concerned with the love of God as it is revealed in various ways, culminating with the words "We read thee best in him who came to bear for us the cross of shame", it also has the lines:

"O heavenly love, how precious still,
In days of weariness and ill,
In nights of pain and helplessness,
To heal, to comfort, and to bless."

So this most active of men had his bad times, which makes these lines doubly helpful.

May I suggest a few hymns which have helped me in this way? You may have quite a different choice, I know:

'My God, how wonderful thou art')
(51 H. & P.)) To help us to meditate
'Father of heaven, whose love) on the mystery of the Godhead
profound' (519 H. & P.))

'Eternal Light!' (458 H. & P.)) To help us meditate on our
) relation with God.

'Thy kingdom come, O God')
(783 H. & P.)) When we are troubled about
'Sing we the King who is) the state of the world.
coming to reign' (244 H. & P.))

'How do thy mercies close me) Evening
round' (562 H. & P.))

'When morning gilds the skies') Morning
(276 H. & P.))

Concerning hymns for meditation in the morning, I have recently rediscovered Charles Wesley's 'Christ, whose glory fills the skies' (457 H. & P.). I have often thought that when primitive man sought an object of worship, what could be more natural than to think of the sun as a deity. To turn to its light and warmth after a night that had been dark and cold would bring an immediate and compelling reaction. (I have not forgotten that a highly-civilised people - the Egyptians - also worshipped the sun.) The prophet Ezekiel condemned sun-worship in the strongest terms (Ezek. 8: 15-18). But elsewhere in Scripture the thought of the sun, with all its life-giving properties as being symbolic of God's love, and his life-giving rays shining on the creatures he has made, is often expressed, e.g. 'The Lord God is a sun . . .' (Psalm 84: 11).

To turn to this great hymn, Wesley echoes Malachi's thought of the Sun of righteousness arising with healing in his rays (Mal. 4: 2), triumphing o'er the shades of night. To dwell on this thought must surely give a lift to the many who cannot get started in the morning. It is a hymn which is appropriate on a dull, wet morning or a bright, sunny one; suitable both when we wake and welcome the day, or when we feel a bit under the weather. There is so much in this hymn that I can only repeat the advice - read it through and meditate on every phrase. Wesley was another great man of incessant activity, yet he needed to pray:

"Pierce the gloom of sin and grief;

• • • • • •

Scatter all my unbelief."

This should encourage each of us when the 'moods' overtake and depress us. We shall return to this great hymn later.

Another rewarding personal exercise - if you have the time to do it (and I now often do have time) - is to try tracing the Biblical quotations on which a hymn is based. Of course, if your hymnal gives you the Scripture from which a verse or a whole hymn is derived, the job is done for you, but even then it is good to look it up and note the differences. For example, 'As pants the hart for cooling streams' (416 H. & P.) is stated to be based on Psalm 42, but if you look up the Psalm you will notice it says nothing about the hart being 'heated in the chase'. We can only think that either Tate or Brady was a hunting man and added this very English interpretation to the original. It refers merely to an animal's normal thirst in a hot country, not to the barbarous practice of hunting it.

In most hymns the Scriptural allusions are more veiled and subtle. I will give two examples, one new and one old. The hymn by Daniel Niles (1908-70), 'Father God in heaven' (518 H. & P.) is stated as being based on the Lord's Prayer. In fact this applies only to the first half, which gives several helpful insights into these familiar words, regrettably at times so carelessly said. I particularly like:

"Kept from Satan's snare
In temptation's hour."

This seems a very cogent version of the much disputed phrase "Lead us not into temptation" (See the reference under 'Hymns we Miss' earlier in this chapter). The words lead on to the author's own thought:

"So from sin set free,
Lord, we seek thy face."

146

This is a thought familiar from the Psalms, Paul's 'children of liberty' (Romans 8: 21), and so on. The beautifully attractive Chinese tune 'Le P'ing' ('Joyous Peace') adds to the magic of this simple yet profound hymn.

The second example, a complete contrast, is Charles Wesley's great hymn already referred to, now thought to have been written to celebrate his conversion and enjoying a new surge of popularity: 'And can it be' (216 H. & P.). I have commented earlier in this chapter on Wesley's gift for expounding on texts in his hymns, and this is surely a good example of his skill. We would not immediately class it as a sacramental hymn, but the opening lines refer us straight back to our Saviour's words at the Last Supper: "This is my blood . . .":

> "And can it be that I should gain
> An interest in the Saviour's blood?"

The end of the verse is reminiscent of Paul's great pronouncements on the Atonement in his Epistle to the Romans. So you could go on through the hymn to the dramatic fourth verse based firmly on Peter's release from prison:

> "My chains fell off, my heart was free,
> I rose, went forth, and followed thee."

Can we also detect echoes of the release of the heroic Paul and Silas as the result of the earthquake at Philippi?

In recent years we have rejoiced in the literal release of hostages from Beirut, each testifying to the power of people's prayers over their years of suffering. Terry Waite, with his firm Christian faith, is the most inspiring example. These thoughts, I think, lead us to Wesley's confidence in God's love which is the theme of the final verse of this great hymn - a string of Paul's most bold and confident claims to the assurance of salvation.

While rejoicing in these recent releases, my mind went back to 1945 when Dietrich Bonhoeffer was imprisoned for his Christian witness and his anti-Nazi activities. Terry Waite eventually had a Bible but Bonhoeffer never did before the day when he was led out to execution. He found this a sore deprivation, but he was able to remember many of the hymns by the great German authors (some of which have appeared in this book). He appears to have been especially indebted to Paul Gerhardt. Was his great hymn "Commit thou all thy griefs" a special help? (672 H. & P.). I would guess he was not only strengthened to meet his death by these hymns but by Scriptural texts that lay behind them. May the sustaining power of these immortal Words of God be always ours.

A similar story, but with a happier ending, concerns Bishop John Wilson of Singapore - how he was imprisoned by the Japanese and frequently interrogated under torture to extract confessions of crimes he had not committed during the 1939-1945 war. He describes his comfortless cell in which there was a tiny window high up. He said "Through this window I could just glimpse the top of the tower of Wesley Church and I was so grateful that that Church had preserved so many of Wesley's hymns. One that I said each day was,

> Christ whose glory fills the skies,
> Christ, the true, the only light,
> Sun of righteousness arise,
> Triumph o'er the shades of night, - - -

The burden of this world was lifted and I was carried into the presence of God."

He was beaten and made to kneel during long questionings and to 'jog his memory' a large iron bar was placed in the crook of his knee joints, making the pain far worse as the weight of his body bore down on it. Just for good measure his guards would jump on this bar from time to time. In the midst of this torture he was taunted "Do you still believe in God." He would reply "I do." "Then why doesn't He save you?" would shout the torturer. John would manage to answer "He does, but not from the pain - He gives me the Spirit to bear it." From time to time he would mutter "Father forgive them" as they took it in turns to flog him. Finally John had the joy of baptising a few - "only a few" he said - who became committed christians, impressed by his *Super*-human courage.

His life after the war as Dean of Manchester and Bishop of Birmingham makes a happy conclusion to this grim period.

These stories of the heroism of men who proved the value and inspiration of hymns in extreme suffering help to prove that in our happy, perhaps humdrum lives these immortal words can be our standby, bringing God, the Father of our Lord Jesus Christ, near to us, by the indwelling of the Holy Spirit.

Bibliography

A few books I have found helpful, which I can recommend to any who want to follow up this subject

The Companion to Hymns and Psalms. Brief, basic, essential; Bible references helpful.

The Penguin Book of Hymns.

A Story before we sing - Davy

Older companions are still valuable:-

The Methodist Hymn Book Illustrated.

Handbook to the Church Hymnary.

The Evolution of the English Hymn - Gillman; etc.

Historical Notes on Hymnals Quoted in this book.

Hymns Ancient and Modern 1861: revised and two supplements added. (Still used in some Churches.) Complete revision 1972.

English Hymnal 1906. Revised 1986.

Methodist Hymn Book, 1904. Good selection but nearly half by the Wesley family.

The Primitive Methodist Hymn Book, 1889; supplement added.

Methodist Hymn Book 1933. Published at Methodist Union. A landmark at this historic occasion. An effort to preserve the best of the previous two books and those of smaller groups. Nearly 1000 hymns including much new material; Destined to last fifty years.

Hymns and Songs 1969 A supplement to the above introducing more new material.

Hymns and Psalms 1983 Prepared by representatives of the Methodist and most of the Free Churches with the object of launching an ecumenical hymnal. A very good book - smaller than predecessors. Unfortunately criticised for omitting many relevant standard hymns; heavy format and wasted space (in music edition).

The B.B.C. Hymn Book (1957).

The Methodist School Hymnal 1911; revised 1939.

INDEX OF HYMNS MENTIONED

151

INDEX OF AUTHORS, COMPOSERS AND SOURCES